Arnold G. Kern –

30: V: 1925.

BY THE SAME WRITER

POEMS (Collected Edition in Two Volumes). 1902.

AN INTRODUCTION TO THE STUDY OF BROWNING 1886, 1906.

AUBREY BEARDSLEY. 1898, 1905.

THE SYMBOLIST MOVEMENT IN LITERATURE. 1899.

PLAYS, ACTING, AND MUSIC. 1903.

CITIES. 1903.

STUDIES IN PROSE AND VERSE. 1904.

SPIRITUAL ADVENTURES. 1905.

THE FOOL OF THE WORLD AND OTHER POEMS. 1906.

STUDIES IN SEVEN ARTS. 1906.

WILLIAM BLAKE. 1907.

CITIES OF ITALY. 1907.

THE ROMANTIC MOVEMENT IN ENGLISH POETRY. 1909.

FIGURES OF SEVERAL CENTURIES. 1916.

CITIES AND SEA-COASTS AND ISLANDS. 1918.

COLOUR STUDIES IN PARIS

STÉPHANE MALLARMÉ
By J. McN. Whistler.

[*Frontispiece.*

COLOUR STUDIES
IN PARIS

BY
ARTHUR SYMONS

LONDON
CHAPMAN AND HALL, Ltd.
1918

TO ISEULT GONNE

*There is a weary, salt, and bitter thing
That eats my heart. I know not what it is.*
                    TRISTAN AND ISEULT: *Act Two.*

CONTENTS

	PAGE
PARIS	3
THE GINGERBREAD FAIR AT VINCENNES	5
MONTMARTRE AND THE LATIN QUARTER	23
PARIS AND IDEAS	39
THE POET OF THE BATS	49
SONGS OF THE STREETS	59
A BOOK OF FRENCH VERSES	67
AT THE AMBASSADEURS	77
YVETTE GUILBERT	79
LA MÉLINITE: MOULIN-ROUGE	91
DANCERS AND DANCING	93
LEON BLOY: THE THANKLESS BEGGAR	105
VICTOR HUGO AND WORDS	115
A TRAGIC COMEDY	127
PÉTRUS BOREL	135

CONTENTS

	PAGE
NOTES ON PARIS AND PAUL VERLAINE	161
THE ABSINTHE-DRINKER	163
AT THE CAFÉ FRANÇOIS PREMIER	165
THE MAN	170
BONHEUR	176
EPIGRAMMES	184
CONFESSIONS	187
DÉDICACES	190
'INVECTIVES'	196
A PRINCE OF COURT PAINTERS	205
ODILON REDON	215

LIST OF ILLUSTRATIONS

	PAGE
STÉPHANE MALLARMÉ, BY WHISTLER	*Frontispiece*
REMY DE GOURMONT, ARTHUR SYMONS, AND HAVELOCK ELLIS . . . . . *To face*	57
ARISTIDE BRUANT . . . . . ,,	59
COVER OF 'LE MIRLITON' . . . ,,	62
YVETTE GUILBERT . . . . ,,	77
YVETTE GUILBERT (CARICATURE) . . ,,	84
FACSIMILE MS. 'LA MÉLINITE' . . .	91, 92
GEORGE SAND . . . . . *To face*	127
PÉTRUS BOREL (MEDALLION) . . . ,,	135
PAUL VERLAINE . . . . . ,,	165
FACSIMILE MS. STÉPHANE MALLARMÉ . ,,	192
FACSIMILE MS. PAUL VERLAINE . . ,,	200

COLOUR STUDIES IN PARIS

PARIS

My Paris is a land where twilight days
Merge into violent nights of black and gold ;
Where, it may be, the flower of dawn is cold :
Ah, but the gold nights, and the scented ways!

Eyelids of women, little curls of hair,
A little nose curved softly, like a shell,
A red mouth like a wound, a mocking veil :
Phantoms, before the dawn, how phantom-fair!

And every woman with beseeching eyes,
Or with enticing eyes, or amorous,
Offers herself, a rose, and craves of us
A rose's place among our memories.

   1894.

THE GINGERBREAD FAIR AT VINCENNES

I

THE tram rolls heavily through the sunshine, on the way to Vincennes. The sun beats on one's head like the glow of a furnace; we are in the second week of May, and the hour is between one and two in the afternoon. From the Place Voltaire, all along the dingy boulevard, there are signs of the fair; first, little stalls, with the refuse of ironmonger and pastry-cook, then little booths, then a few roundabouts, the wooden horses standing motionless. At the Place de la Nation we have reached the fair itself. Already the roundabouts swarm in gorgeous inactivity: shooting-galleries with lofty names—Tir Metropolitan, Tir de Lutèce—lead on to the establishments of *cochonnerie*, the gingerbread pigs, which have given its name to the *Foire au pain d'épice.* From between the two pillars, each with its airy statue, we can look right on, through lanes of stalls and alleys of dusty trees, to the railway bridge which crosses the other end of the Cours de Vincennes, just before it subsides into the desolate Boulevard Soult and the impoverished grass of the ramparts. Hardly anyone passes: the fair, which is up late, sleeps till three. I saunter slowly along, watching the drowsy attitudes of the women behind their stalls, the men who lounge beside their booths. Only the photographer is in activity, and as you pause a moment to note his collection of grimacing and lachrymose likenesses (probably very like), a framed horror is thrust into your hand, and a voice insinuates: *Six pour un sou, Monsieur!*

To stroll through the fair just now is to have a sort of "Private View." The hour of disguises has not yet begun. The heavy girl who, in an hour's time, will pose in rosy tights and cerulean tunic on those trestles yonder in front of the theatre, sits on the ladder-staircase of her "jivin wardo," her "living waggon," as the gipsies call it, diligently mending, with the help of scissors and thread, a piece of canvas which is soon to be a castle or a lake. A lion-tamer in his shirt-sleeves is chatting with the proprietress of a collection of waxworks. A fairy queen is washing last week's tights in a great tub. And booths and theatres seem to lounge in the same *déshabille*. With their vacant platforms, their closed doors, their too visible masterpieces of coloured canvas, they stand, ugly and dusty, every crack and patch exposed by the pitiless downpour of the sunlight. Here is the show of Pezon, the old lion-tamer, who is now assisted by his son; opposite, his rival and constant neighbour, Bidel. The Grand Théâtre Cocherie announces its *grand féerie* in three acts and twenty tableaux. A *concert international* succeeds a very dismal-looking *Temple de la Gaieté*. Here is the *Théâtre Macketti;* here the *Grande Musée Vivant;* here a *Galerie artistique* at one sou. *Laurent, inimitable dompteur (pour la première fois à Paris)* has for companion *Juliano et ses fauves: Fosse aux Lions*. There is a very large picture of a Soudanese giant —*il est ici, le géant Soudanais; 2m. 20 de hauteur*—outside a very small tent; the giant, very black in the face, and very red as to his habiliments, holds a little black infant in the palm of his hand, and by his side, carefully avoiding (by a delicacy of the painter) a too direct inspection, stands a gendarme, who extends five fingers in a gesture of astonishment, somewhat out of keeping with the perfect placidity of his face. *Théâtres des Illusions* flourish side by side with *Musées artistiques*, in which the latest explosive Anarchist, or *Le double crime du boulevard du Temple* is the "great attraction" of the moment. Highly coloured and freely designed pictures of nymphs and naiads are accompanied by such seductive and ingenious recommendations as this, which I copy textually. I cannot reproduce the emphasis of the lettering:

Etoiles Animées. Filles de l'Air. Nouvelle attraction par le professeur Julius. Pourquoi Mlle. Isaure est-elle appelée Déesse des Eaux? C'est par sa grâce et son pouvoir mystérieux de paraître au milieu des Eaux limpides, devant tous les spectateurs qui deviendront ses Admirateurs. En Plein Théâtre la belle Isaure devient Syrène et Nayade! charme par ses jeux sveltes et souples, apparait en

Plein Mer, et présentée par le professeur Julius à chaque représentation. Plusieurs pâles imitateurs essayent de copier la belle Isaure, mais le vrai Public, amateur du Vrais et du Beau, dira que la Copie ne vaut pas l'original. And there is a *Jardin mystérieux* which represents an improbable harem, with an undesirable accompaniment of performing reptiles. Before this tent I pause, but not for the sake of its announcement; in the doorway sits a beautiful young girl of about sixteen, a Jewess, with a face that Leonardo might have painted. A red frock reaches to her knees, her thin legs, in white tights, are crossed nonchalantly: in her black hair there is the sparkle of false diamonds, ranged in a tiara above the gracious contour of her forehead; and she sits there, motionless, looking straight before her with eyes that see nothing, absorbed in some vague reverie, the Monna Lisa of the Gingerbread Fair.

II

It is half-past three, and the Cours de Vincennes is a carnival of colours, sounds and movements. Looking from the Place de la Nation, one sees a long thin line of customers along the stalls of bonbons and gingerbread, and the boulevard has the air of a black-edged sheet of paper, until the eye reaches a point where the shows begin. Then the crowd is seen in black patches, sometimes large, extending half across the road, sometimes small; every now and then one of the black patches thins rapidly as the people mount the platform, or there is a simultaneous movement from one point of attraction to another. At one's back the roundabouts are squealing the *répertoire Paulus*, in front there is a continuous deafening rumble of drums, with an inextricable jangle and jumble of brass bands, each playing a different tune, all at once, and all close together. Shrill or hoarse voices are heard for a moment, to be drowned the next by the intolerable drums and cornets. As one moves slowly down the long avenue, distracted by the cries, the sounds, coming from both sides at once, it is quite another aspect that is presented by those dingy platforms, those gaping canvases of but an hour ago. Every platform is alive with human

GINGERBREAD FAIR AT VINCENNES

frippery. A clown in reds and yellows, with a floured and rouged face, bangs a big drum, an orchestra (sometimes of one, sometimes of fifteen) "blows through brass" with the full power of its lungs; fulgently and scantily attired ladies throng the foreground, a man in plain clothes squanders the remains of a voice in howling the attractions of the interior, and in the background, at a little table, an opulent lady sits at the receipt of custom, with the business-like solemnity of the *dame du comptoir* of a superior restaurant. Occasionally there is a *pas seul*, more often an indifferent waltz, at times an impromptu comedy. Outside Bidel's establishment a tired and gentle dromedary rubs its nose against the pole to which it is tied; elsewhere a monkey swings on a trapeze; a man addresses the crowd with a snake about his shoulders, and my Monna Lisa, too, has twined a snake around her, and stands holding the little malevolent head in her fingers, like an exquisite and harmless Medusa.

Under the keen sunlight every colour stands out sharply, and to pass between those two long lines of gesticulating figures is to plunge into an orgy of clashing colours. All the women wear the coarsest of worsted tights, the usual tint of which is intended to be flesh-colour, but it varies, through all the shades, from the palest of pink to the brightest of red. Often the tights are patched, sometimes they are not even patched. The tunic may be mauve, or orange, or purple, or blue; it is generally open in front, showing a close-fitting jersey of the same colour as the tights. The arms are bare, the faces, as a rule, made up with discretion and restraint. There is one woman, who must once have been very beautiful, who appears in ballet skirts; there is a man in blue-grey cloak and hood, warriors in plumes and cuirass; but for the most part it is the damsels in flesh-coloured tights and jerseys who parade on the platforms outside the theatres. When they break into a waltz it is always the most dissonant of mauves, and pinks, and purples that choose one another as partners. As the girls move carelessly and clumsily round in the dance, they continue the absorbing conversations in which they are mostly engaged. Rarely does anyone show the slightest interest in the crowd whose eyes are all fixed — so thirstingly! — upon them. They stand or move as they are told, mechanically, indifferently, and that is all. Often, but not always, well-formed, they have occasionally pretty faces as well. There is a brilliant little creature, who forms one of the crowd of warriors outside the Théâtre Cocherie, who has quite an individual type of charm and intelligence. She has a boyish face, little black curls on her forehead, a proud, sensitive mouth, and black eyes full of wit and defiance. As Miss Angelina, *artiste gymnasiarque équilibriste et danseuse*, goes through a very ordinary selection of steps ("rocks," "scissors," and the like, as they are called in the profession), Julienne's eyes devour every movement; she is learning how to do it, and will practise it herself without telling anyone, until she can surprise them some day by taking Miss Angelina's place.

III

But it is at night, towards nine o'clock, that the fair is at its best. The painted faces, the crude colours, assume their right aspect, become harmonious, under the artificial light. The dancing pinks and reds whirl on the platforms, flash into the gaslight, disappear for an instant into a solid shadow, against the light, emerge vividly. The moving black masses surge to and fro before the booths; from the side one sees lines of rigid figures, faces that the light shows in eager profile. Outside the Théâtre Cocherie there is a shifting light which turns a dazzling glitter, moment by moment, across the road; it plunges like a sword into one of the trees opposite, casts a glow as of white fire over the transfigured green of leaves and branches, and then falls off, baffled by the impenetrable leafage. As the light drops suddenly on the crowd, an instant before only dimly visible, it throws into fierce relief the intent eyes, the gaping mouths, the unshaven cheeks, darting into the hollows of broken teeth, pointing cruelly at every scar and wrinkle. At every return it dazzles the eyes of one tall girl at the end of the platform, among the warriors; she turns away her head, or grimaces. In the middle of the platform there is a violent episode of horse-play; a man in plain clothes belabours two clowns with a

GINGERBREAD FAIR AT VINCENNES

sounding lath, and is in turn belaboured; then the three rush together pell-mell, roll over one another, bump down the steps to the ground, return, recommence, with the vigour and gusto of schoolboys in a scrimmage. Further on a white clown tumbles on a stage, girls in pink, and black, and white move vaguely before a dark red curtain, brilliant red breeches sparkle, a girl *en garçon*, standing at one side in a graceful pose which reveals her fine outlines, shows a motionless silhouette, cut out sharply against the light; the bell rings, the drum beats, a large blonde-wigged woman, dressed in Louis XIV costume, cries her wares and holds up placards, white linen with irregular black lettering. Outside a boxing booth a melancholy lean man blows inaudibly into a horn; his cheeks puff, his fingers move, but not a sound can be heard above the thunder of the band of Laurent le Dompteur. Before the *ombres chinoises* a lamp hanging to a tree sheds its light on a dark red background, on the gendarme who moves across the platform, on the pink and green hat of madame, and on her plump hand supporting her chin, on monsieur's irreproachable silk hat and white whiskers. Near by is a theatre where they are giving the *Cloches de Corneville*, and the platform is thronged with lounging girls in tights. They turn their backs unconcernedly to the crowd, and the light falls on pointed shoulderblades, one distinguishes the higher vertebræ of the spine. A man dressed in a burlesque female costume kicks a print dress extravagantly into the air, flutters a ridiculous fan, with mincing airs, with turns and somersaults. People begin to enter, and the platform clears; a line of figures marches along the narrow footway running the length of the building, to a curtained entrance at the end. The crowd in front melts away, straggles across the road to another show, straggling back again as the drum begins to beat and the line of figures marches back to the stage.

In front, at the outskirts of the crowd, two youngsters in blouses have begun to dance, kicking their legs in the air to the strains of a mazurka; and now two women circle. A blind man, in the space between two booths, sits holding a candle in his hand, a pitiful object; the light falls on his straw hat, the white placard on his breast, his face is in shadow. As I pause before a booth where a fat woman in tights flourishes a pair of boxing gloves, I find myself by the side of my Monna Lisa of the enchanted garden. Her show is over, and she is watching the others. She wears a simple black dress and a dark blue apron; her hair is neatly tied back with a ribbon. She is quite ready to be amused, and it is not only I, but the little professional lady, who laughs at the farce which begins on a neighbouring stage, where a patchwork clown comes out arm in arm with a nightmare of a pelican, the brown legs very human, the white body and monstrous orange bill very fearsome and fantastic. A pale Pierrot languishes against a tree: I see him as I turn to go, and, looking back, I can still distinguish the melancholy figure above the waltz of the red, and pink, and purple under the lights, the ceaseless turning of those human dolls, with their fixed smile, their painted colours.

IV

It is half-past eleven, and the fair is over for the night. One by one the lights are extinguished; faint glimmers appear in the little square windows of dressing-rooms and sleeping-rooms; silhouettes cross and re-cross the drawn blinds, with lifted arms and huddled draperies. The gods of *tableaux vivants*, negligently modern in attire, stroll off across the road to find a comrade, rolling a cigarette between their fingers. Monna Lisa passes rapidly, with her brother, carrying a marketing basket. And it is a steady movement townwards; the very stragglers prepare to go, stopping, from time to time, to buy a great gingerbread pig with Jean or Suzanne scrawled in great white letters across it. Outside one booth, not yet closed, I am arrested by the desolation of a little frail creature, with a thin, suffering, painted face, his pink legs crossed, who sits motionless by the side of the great drum, looking down wearily at the cymbals that he still holds in his hands. In the open spaces roundabouts turn, turn, a circle of moving lights, encircled by a thin line of black shadows. The sky darkens, a little wind is rising; the night, after this day of heat, will be stormy. And still, to the waltz measure of the roundabouts, turning, turning frantically, the last lingerers defy the midnight, a dance of shadows.

1896.

MONTMARTRE AND THE
LATIN QUARTER

MONTMARTRE AND THE LATIN QUARTER

Of all places for a holiday, Paris, to my mind, is the most recreative; but not the Paris of the English tourist. To the English tourist Paris consists in the Champs-Elysées and the Grands Boulevards, with, of course, the shops in the Rue de Rivoli. In other words, he selects out of all Paris precisely what is least Parisian. The Rue de Rivoli always reminds me of Boulogne; the one is the Englishman's part of Paris, as the other is the Englishman's part of France, and their further resemblances are many and intimate. The Champs-Elysées have their moments and their hours of interest; it may be admitted that they are only partially Anglicised. As for the Grands Boulevards, which are always, certainly, attractive to any genuine lover of cities, to any real amateur of crowds, they

are, after all, not Parisian, but cosmopolitan.
They are simply the French equivalent of
that great, complex, inextricable concourse
of people which we find instinctively crowding, in London, along Piccadilly; in Berlin,
down the Unter den Linden; in Madrid, over
the Prado; in Venice, about the Piazza: a
crowding of people who have come together
from all the ends of the earth, who have, if
tourist likes to meet tourist, mutual attraction
enough; who have, undoubtedly, the curiosity
of an exhibition or an ethnological museum;
but from whom you will never learn the
characteristics of the country in which you
find them. What is really of interest in a
city or in a nation is not that which it has,
however differentiated, in common with other
nations and cities, but that which is unique
in it, the equivalent of which you will search
for in vain elsewhere. Now the two parts
of Paris which are unique, the equivalent of
which you will search for in vain elsewhere,
are the Quartier Latin and Montmartre.
And these are just the quarters which the
English tourist, as a rule, knows least about;
fancying, though he may, that he knows

them, because he has climbed Montmartre as far as the Moulin-Rouge, and gone leftward one Saturday night as far as Bullier.

I have often, when sitting at the Brasserie d'Harcourt, on the "les serious" side, the side facing the Boulevard Saint-Michel, tried to imagine that gay, noisy, and irresponsible throng which surges in and out of the doors, overflows the *terrasse*, and scatters up and down the street; I have tried, but always in vain, to imagine it, so to speak, in terms of London. No, it is simply unthinkable. That Piccadilly (or is it to be the Strand?) will some day more or less approximate to the continental idea of the necessary comforts of life, that it will have its cafés like every other civilised city, and so redeem England from the disgrace of being the only country where men have to drink, like cattle, standing; that, I have no doubt, is merely a matter of time; it will come. But there will never be a Boul' Mich' in London. It is as impossible as Marcelle and Suzanne. The Boul' Mich' is simply the effervescence of irrepressible youth; and youth in London never effervesces, or only in one man here, in one woman there. The stern British moralist tells us it is indeed fortunate that we have not a Boulevard Saint-Michel in our midst; that we have not, and never can have, a d'Harcourt; and he points to the vice which flaunts there. No doubt whatever vice is to be found in the Quartier, does very much flaunt itself. But is it not really less vicious, in a certain sense, than the corresponding thing in London, which takes itself so seriously as well as cautiously, is so self-convinced of evil-doing and has all the unhealthy excitement of an impotent but persistent Puritan conscience? However, be this as it may, the real peculiarity of the youth of the Latin Quarter is its friendly gaiety, its very boisterous sociability, its extraordinary capacity for prolonging the period of its existence— the existence of that volatile quantity, youth —into the period of beards and the past thirties. You may say, if you like, that it is ridiculous, that grown-up men should know better than to run about the street with long hair and large hats, singing and shouting from eleven in the evening till two in the morning. It has its ridiculous side, certainly, but it is

MONTMARTRE AND LATIN QUARTER 27

remarkable, above all, as a survival of youth, and it implies a *joie de vivre*, which is a very valuable and not a very common quality.

The place and the moment where the Quartier Latin becomes—what shall I say?—its best self, are upon those fine Sunday afternoons when the band plays in the Luxembourg Gardens. Does everyone know Manet's picture of the scene: the long frock-coats, the long hair, the very tall hats, the voluminous skirts of the ladies, and the enchantment of those green trees over and between and around it all? Well, the real thing is as delightful even as a Manet; and when I am in Paris, in the fine weather, I consider that Sunday is not quite Sunday if a part of it is not spent just as those people in the picture spend it. Early in the afternoon groups begin to form; Marcelle and Suzanne bring their sewing, or a book of verses, for a pretence, and each has her little circle about her. The chairs around the band-stand fill gradually, the tables of the little green *buvette* spread further and further outwards, leaving just room for the promenade which will soon begin, that church-parade of such another sort from the London one, so blithely—

> within this fair,
> This quiet church of leaves.

Further out again, along the terrace, between the last trees and the line and curve of the balustrade, there is an outer, quite different, rim of mothers and nurses and children. And now the band is playing, it is the ballet music in *Faust*; and the shimmery music, coming like sunshine into the sunlights of such an afternoon, just here and now, sounds almost beautiful, as things do always when they are beautifully in keeping. Marcelle and Suzanne, between two shouts of laughter, feel the poetry of the moment; they are even silent, biting meditatively the corner of a fanciful handkerchief. And the slowly moving throng which trails around the narrow alley between the chairs is no longer the noisy, irrepressible throng which last night acted the farce of the *monôme* from door to door of the d'Harcourt; it is the other, more serious, more sentimental side of that vivid youth which incarnates and is the incarnation of the Quartier Latin.

Up at Montmartre, how different is the

atmosphere, yet how typically Parisian! To reach Montmartre you have to go right through Paris, and I always think the route followed by that charming omnibus, the " Batignolles-Clichy-Odéon," shows one more of Paris, in the forty or fifty minutes that it takes, than any other route I know. It is an April evening; nine o'clock has just struck. I am tired of turning over the books under the arcades of the Odéon, and I mount the omnibus. The heavy wheels rattle over the rough stones, down the broad, ugly Rue de Tournon. We curve through narrow, winding streets, which begin to grow Catholic, blossoming out into windowfuls of wax-candles, as we near Saint-Sulpice, our first stopping-place. After we have left the broad, always somewhat prim and quiet open space, dominated by the formidable bulk of the curious, composite church, it is by more or less featureless ways that we reach the Boulevard Saint-Germain, coming out suddenly under the trees, so beautiful, I always think, in that odd, acute glitter which gas-light gives them. There are always a good many people waiting here; my side of the imperial is soon full. We cross the road, and the two horses start at full speed, as they invariably do at that particular place, down the Rue des Saints-Pères. The street is long and narrow, few people are passing; all the life of the street seems to be concentrated behind those lighted windows, against which we pass so close. I catch a glimpse of interiors; a table with a red table-cloth, a lamp upon it, a girl sewing; she leans forward, and the lights crimson her cheek. Another room, an old woman holding a candle moves across the window; in another I see the back of an arm-chair, just a tuft of blonde hair overtopping it; there are two candles on the table, several books. Farther on, the curtains are drawn, I can see only a silhouette, the face and bust of a woman, clearly outlined, as she sits motionless. We turn the corner, are on the *Quai*, and now crossing slowly the Pont des Arts. The heavy masonry of the Louvre looms up in front; to right and left below, the Seine, draped in shadow, with sharp points of white and red where the lights strike the water. Then begins the jolting and rumbling over the horrible pavement of the Louvre, the sudden silence as the wheels glide over the *asphalte*, and we emerge, through that impossibly narrow archway, into the Rue de Rivoli; in two minutes we are at the Palais Royal. For a moment I see the twisting currents of cabs, down the Avenue de l'Opéra, and then we are in the interminable Rue de Richelieu, broken only by the long, but new, monotony of the dreary Bibliothèque Nationale, and that odd, charming little square opposite, with its old houses, its fountain, its dingy trees, its seats. At last we have reached the Grands Boulevards, and we edge our way slowly across, between the omnibuses and cabs. The boulevard is not crowded, it is the hour of the theatres; and then I am facing that side of the street which I never care for, the virtuous side (despite Julien's). When we turn up the Rue Le Peletier, out of the broad, lighted space stretching on in a long vista between the trees and lamp-posts, we find ourselves, ere long, in a new atmosphere; first, that ambiguous quarter of the Chaussée d'Antin, then the franker Montmartre. As we toil up the steep Rue Notre-Dame-de-Lorette, past that severe but

eccentric church which seems trying to block
our way, but in vain, I watch curiously the
significant windows, with their lights and
their blinds. As the horses turn aside, Clichy-
wards, I get down; there, just before me, as
if at the other end of the street, across the
broad open space of the Place Blanche, are
the red bulk and waving sails of the Moulin-
Rouge. And that is one of the landmarks
of Montmartre.

They tell me that Montmartre is not what
it once was, in the great days of the Château-
Rouge, of the Boule-Noire. And even in my
time there has been a certain falling away;
for have I not seen the death of the Elysée-
Montmartre, and the trivial resurrection, out
of its ashes, of a certain characterless Trianon-
Concert?

Still, if some of the glories of Montmartre
are gone, Montmartre remains, and it remains
unique. In no other city can I recall anything
in itself so sordidly picturesque as those crawl-
ing heights, which lead up to the Butte, so
wonderful as the vision of the city which the
Butte gives one. I know Montmartre chiefly
by night; it is not a place for the day; and

the view of Paris which I am thinking of is the view of Paris by night. When you have climbed as high as you can climb, ending almost with ladders, you reach a dreary little strip of ground, in which a rough wooden paling seems to hold you back from falling sheer into the abyss of Paris. Under a wild sky, as I like to see it, the city floats away endlessly, a vague, immense vision of forests of houses, softened by fringes of actual forest; here and there a dome, a tower, brings suddenly before the eyes a definite locality; but for the most part it is but a succession of light and shade, here tall white houses coming up out of a pit of shadow, there an unintelligible mass of darkness, sheared through by an inexplicable arrow of light. Right down below, one looks straight into the lighted windows, distinguishing the outline of the lamp on the table, of the figure which moves about the room; while, in the far distance, there is nothing but a faint, reddish haze, rising dubiously into the night, as if the lusts of Paris smoked to the skies. Night after night I have been up to this odd, fascinating little corner, merely to look at all I had left behind; and I have been struck by the attraction which this view obviously has for the somewhat unpleasant and unimpressionable people who inhabit the neighbourhood. Aristide Bruant's heroes and heroines, the lady on her way to Saint-Lazare, the gentleman—who knows?—perhaps to La Roquette, they rest from their labours at times, and, leaning over the wooden paling, I am sure enjoy Paris impressionistically. Perhaps this is one of the gifts of the *esprit Montmartre*, that philosophy of the pavement which has always been more or less localised in this district. Here at Montmartre of course, and of it essentially, are almost all the public balls, the really Parisian café-concerts, which exist in Paris. The establishments in the Champs-Elysées are after an order of their own; the Folies-Bergère is an unsuccessful attempt to imitate an English music-hall, and a successful attempt to attract the English public; but amusing Paris, and Paris which amuses itself, goes to Montmartre. The cabaret of Aristide Bruant has lost something of its special character since Bruant took to singing at the Ambassadeurs; the Concert Lisbonne, which was once so pleasantly eccentric, has become ordinary; but there is still the true ring of Montmartre in the Carillon, that homely little place in the Rue de la Tour-d'Auvergne, and the baser kind of Montmartre wit in the Concert des Concierges, not far off. And then, to end the evening, is there not the Rat Mort, of which a conscientious English lady novelist once gave so fanciful a picture? The Rat Mort, which ends the evening, sums up Montmartre; not wisely, perhaps, not prudently, but with "some emotions and a moral."

1904.

PARIS AND IDEAS

PARIS AND IDEAS

I HAVE been turning over a book which has called up many memories, and which has set me thinking about people and ideas. The book is called *French Portraits: being Appreciations of the Writers of Young France*, is published in Boston and it is written by an American, who writes somewhat hysterically, but in a spirit of generous appreciation. It is pretentious, as the people in the Latin Quarter are pretentious; that is to say, innocently, and on behalf of ideas. It all keeps step, gallantly enough, to a march, not Schumann's, of the followers of David against the Philistines. One seems to see a straggling company wandering down at night from the heights of Montmartre: the thin faces, long hair, flat-brimmed tall hats and wide-brimmed soft hats, the broken gestures, eager voices, desperate light-heartedness. They have not more talent than people over here; they are much more likely to waste, as it is called, whatever talent they have; but these people whom this book calls up before us are after all the enthusiasts of ideas, and their follies bubble up out of a drunkenness at least as much spiritual as material. Few of the idealists I have known have been virtuous; that is to say, they have chosen their virtues after a somewhat haphazard plan of their own; some of them have loved absinthe, others dirt, all idleness; but why expect everything at once? Have we, who lack ideas and ideals, enough of the solid virtues to put into the balance against these weighty abstractions? I only ask the question; but I persist in thinking that we have still a great deal to learn from Paris, and especially on matters of the higher morality.

Well, this writer, in his vague, heated, liberal way, scatters about him, in this large book of his, many excellent criticisms of people and things; flinging them in our faces, indeed, and as often the stem without the flower as the flower without the stem. He tells us about Verlaine and Mallarmé, about Barrès, Marcel Schwob, Maeterlinck, Moréas, Pierre Louÿs, and a score of others; not as precisely as one might have wished, often indeed rather misleadingly, but always with at least the freshness of a personal interest. An unwary reader might, it is true, imagine that the chapter on Maeterlinck records an actual conversation, an actual walk through Brussels: instead of a conversation wholly imaginary, made up of scraps out of the essays, rather casually tossed together. Such a reader will indeed be beset by pitfalls, and will perhaps come away with several curious impressions: such as that Adolphe Retté is a great poet and Henri de Régnier not a poet at all. But books are not written for unwary readers, and pitfalls are only dangerous to those who have not the agility to avoid them. The portraits, especially Valloton's clever outlines (mostly reproduced from Remy de Gourmont's two admirable volumes of *Le Livre des Masques*), give a serious value to these pages, and there are, in all, more than fifty portraits.

As I turn over the pictures, recognising face after face, I am reminded of many nights and days during the ten years that I have known Paris, and a wheel of memory seems to turn in my head like a kaleidoscope, flashing out the pictures of my own that I keep there. The great sleepy and fiery head of Verlaine is in so many of them. He lies back in his corner at the Café François Premier, with his eyes half shut; he drags on my arm as we go up the boulevard together; he shows me his Bible in the little room up the back stairs; he nods his nightcap over a great picture book as he sits up in bed at the hospital. I see Mallarmé as he opens the door to me on that fourth floor of the Rue de Rome, with his exquisite manner of welcome. Catulle Mendès lectures on the poetry of the Parnassians, reading Glatigny's verses with his suave and gliding intonation. I see Maeterlinck in all the hurry of a departure, between two portmanteaus; Marcel Schwob in a quiet corner by his own fireside, discussing the first quarto of *Hamlet*. Maurice Barrès stands before an after-luncheon camera, with the Princess Mathilde on his arm, in an improvised group on the lawn. Jean Moréas, with his practical air, thunders out a poem of his own to a waitress in a Bouillon Duval. I find myself by the side of Adolphe Retté at a strange performance in which a play of Tola Dorian is followed by a play of Rachilde. Stuart Merrill introduces me to an editor at the Bullier, Vielé-Griffin speaks English with an evident reluctance at the office of the *Mercure de France*, where Henri de Régnier is silent under his eye-glass. It is a varied company, and there are all the others whom I do not know, or whom I have met only out of Paris, like Verhaeren. In those houses, those hospitals, those cafés, many of the ideas on which, consciously or unconsciously, how many of us are now living, came into existence. Meanwhile, how many ideas, of any particular importance to anybody, have come into existence in the London drawing-rooms and clubs of the period, where our men of letters meet one another, with a mutually comfortable resolve not to talk "shop"?

Ideas, it may be objected, are one thing; achievement is quite another. Yes, achievement is quite another, but achievement may sometimes be left out of the question not unprofitably. It is too soon to see how much has been actually done by the younger men I have named; but think how Maeterlinck has brought a new soul into the drama; has brought (may one not say?) the soul into drama. Think what Verlaine has done for French poetry, ending a tradition, which only waited extinction, and creating in its place a new law of freedom, of legitimate freedom, full of infinite possibilities. And, coming down to the very youngest school of "Naturists" (or is there, as I write, a still younger one already?), is there not a significant ferment of thought, a convinced and persuasive restatement of great principles, which every generation has to discover over again for itself, under some new form? All these men, or, to be exact, nearly all these men, have thought before writing, have thought about writing, have thought about other things than writing. They have taken the trouble to form theories, they have not hesitated to lay a foundation before building. The foundation has not always been solid, nor the building a fine piece of architecture. But at least literature in France is not a mere professional business, as so much of what passes for literature is in England, it is not written for money, and it is not written mechanically, for the mere sake of producing a book of verse or prose. In Paris the word art means a very serious and a very definite thing : a thing for which otherwise very unheroic people will cheerfully sacrifice whatever chances they may have of worldly success. Over here I know remarkably few people who seem to me to be sacrificing as much for art as almost any one of those disorderly young men who walk so picturesquely in the Luxembourg Gardens when the band plays. Well, the mere desire to excel, the mere faithfulness to a perhaps preposterous theory of one's duty to art, the mere attempt to write literature, is both an intellectual and a moral quality, which it is worth while to recognise for what it is worth, even if the outcome of it, for the moment, should but be some *Père Ubu* in all the shapelessness of the embryo. Where we have the germ of life, life will in time work out its own accomplishment. And for ideas, which are the first stirrings of life about to begin, we must still, I think, look to France.

1900.

THE POET OF THE BATS

THE POET OF THE BATS

Visitors to the Salon du Champ de Mars cannot fail to have noticed a full-length portrait by Whistler, the portrait of a gentleman of somewhat uncertain age, standing in an attitude half chivalrous, half funambulesque, his hand lightly posed on a small cane. There is something distinguished, something factitious, about the whole figure, and on turning to the catalogue one could not but be struck by a certain fantastic appropriateness in the name, Comte Robert de Montesquiou-Fezensac, even if that name conveyed no further significance. To those who know something of the curiosities of French literary society, the picture has its interest as a portrait of the oddest of Parisian "originals," the typical French "æsthete," from whose cult of the hortensia Oscar Wilde no doubt learnt the worship of the sunflower; while to readers of Huysmans it has the further interest of being a portrait of the real des Esseintes, the hero of that singular and remarkable romance of the Decadence, *A Rebours*. It is scarcely likely that many of the people, or indeed any of the English people who saw the picture, knew that it was also the portrait of a poet, the poet of the bats, *Les Chauves-Souris*, an enormous volume of five hundred closely printed pages.

The Comte de Montesquiou, though living, and a personage, and of late a *fait divers* in the papers for purely mundane reasons, is none the less a legendary being, of whom all the stories that are told may very likely be true, of whom at all events nothing can be told more fantastic than the truth. Has he, or had he, really a series of rooms, draped in different tones, in one of which he could only read French, in another only Latin? Did he really gild the back of the tortoise, and then inlay it with jewels, so that it might crawl over the carpet in arabesques of living colour, until the poor beast died of the burden of its unwonted splendour? Did he really invent an orchestra of perfumes, an orchestra of liqueurs, on which he could play the subtlest harmonies of the senses? He certainly at one time possessed an incredible wardrobe, from which he would select and combine, with infinite labour, the costume of the day; apologising, on a certain misty afternoon, for not employing the Scotch symphony which had once before so perfectly suited a similar day: "but it takes my servant so long to prepare it!" On one occasion a distinguished French writer, one of the most recent of Academicians, was astonished, on opening a letter from the Comte de Montesquiou, to find along with the letter a manuscript copy of Balzac's *Curé de Tours*, written in an illiterate hand. Nothing whatever was said about it, and on meeting his correspondent, the Academician inquired if it was by oversight that the manuscript had been enclosed. "Oh, no," was the answer, "the fact is, my cook and my butler are always quarrelling, and in order to occupy them and keep them out of mischief, I give them Balzac's stories to copy out; and I send the copies to my friends. *Père Goriot* I sent to Leconte de Lisle: I only sent you a short one."

Until a year or two ago, the Comte de Montesquiou indulged in the luxury of enjoying an artistic reputation without having done anything, or at least without having published. It was known that he wrote poems, but no one had seen them; he had resolved to out-Mallarmé Mallarmé, and he succeeded so well that it was generally supposed that these vague, shrouded poems were the quintessence of what was perversely exquisite in spirit and in form, probably few in number, but no doubt not less faultless than original. All at once the veil was dropped; the huge volume of the *Chauves-Souris* appeared, and the reticent and mysterious poet was found soliciting press-notices, paying actresses to recite his poems, giving receptions at his "Pavillion" at Versailles, and buttonholing distinguished poets, to ask them what they really thought of his poems. It is a little difficult to say what one thinks of these poems. They are divided, according to an apparently rigid but entirely unintelligible plan, into a great many divisions, of which these are the principal: *Zaimph, Demi-Teintes* (*Préludes*), *Ténèbres* (*Interludes*), *Bêtes et*

THE POET OF THE BATS

Gens (*Ombres Chinoises*), *Pénombres Office de la Lune* (*Litanies et Antiennes*), *Clairière* (*Coryphées*), *Jets de Feu et Eaux d'Artifice* (*Aqua-Teintes*), *Lunatiques, Vieilles Lunes et Lunes Rousses, Candidates* (*Néomenies*), *Syzygie* (*Ombre portée*), *Ancien Régime*. All this is supposed to represent "une concentration du mystère nocturne," and a prose commentary, which certainly makes darkness more visible, is added, because, the author tells us, "des sollicitudes amies veulent qu'un léger fil permette à des esprits curieux et bienveillants de reconnaître vite le labyrinthe, et, plus expressément, d'apprécier la division architectonique, voire architecturale, peut-être le meilleur mérite du poème." Probably nothing more calmly crazy than this book—in which there is all the disorder without any of the delirium of madness—was ever written: the book certainly has its interest. The possibilities of verse for the expression of fluent, contorted, and interminable nonsense have never been more cogently demonstrated than in the pages from which I cull at random these two stanzas:

> Terreur des Troglôdytès,
> Sur leurs tapis de Turquies,
> Et de tous les rats de tes
> Batrakhomyomakhyes,
>
> Homère : Méridarpax,
> Voleur de portioncule ;
> Trôxartès et Psikharpax,
> Par qui Péléiôn recule.

This is quite an average specimen of the manner of the poet of the bats : if, however, one prefers a greater simplicity, we need but turn the page, and we read :

> La nuit tous les chats sont gris,
> Toutes les souris sont fauves :
> Chauves-souris et chat-chauves,
> Chats-chauves chauves-souris !

It is not a quality that the author would probably appreciate, but the quality that most impresses in this book is the extraordinary diligence that must have been required to produce it. There is not a spontaneous verse in it, from beginning to end few would seem to have required thought, but none could have failed to demand labour. At its best it has that funambulesque air of the Whistler portrait ; when it is not playing tricks it is ambling along stolidly ; but the quintessential des Esseintes, the father and child of the Decadence, well, des Esseintes has no rival to fear in the merely real Comte Robert de Montesquiou-Fezensac.

1895.

[*To face p.* 57.

SONGS OF THE STREETS

Pour Monsieur Arthur Symons
A. Bruant
1892

[*To face p.* 59.

SONGS OF THE STREETS

THE verse of Aristide Bruant, written, as it is, to be sung, and before the casual and somewhat disorderly audience of a small *cabaret* near what was once the Elysée-Montmartre; written, as it is, mainly in the slang of the quarter, the uncomely *argot* of those *boulevards extérieurs* which are the haunts of all that is most sordidly depraved in Paris,—this verse is yet, in virtue of its rare qualities of simplicity, sincerity, and poignant directness, verse of really serious, and not inconsiderable, literary merit. Like the powerful designs of Steinlen, which illustrate them, these songs are for the most part ugly enough, they have no charm or surprise of sentiment, they appeal to one by no imported elegances, by none of the conventionalities of pathos or pity. They take the real life of poor and miserable and vicious people, their real sentiments, their typical moments of emotion or experience—as in the very terrible and very blasphemous song of the rain, and the poor soaked vagabond ready to "curse God and die"—and they say straight out, in the fewest words, just what such people would really say, with a wonderful art in the reproduction of the actual vulgar accent. Take, for instance, the thief, shut up *à Mazas*, who writes to his *p'tit' Rose*, asking her to send him *un peu d'oseille* (a little "oof"):

> Tu dois ben ça à ton p'tit homme
> Qu'a p't'êt' été méchant pour toi,
> Mais qui t'aimait ben, car, en somme,
> Si j'te flaupais, tu sais pourquoi.
> A présent qu'me v'là dans les planques
> Et qu'je n'peux pus t'coller des tas,
> Tu n'te figur's pas c'que tu m'manques,
>   A Mazas.
>
> Faut que j'te d'mande encor' que qu'chose,
> Ça s'rait qu' t'aill's voir un peu mes vieux.
> Vas-y, dis, j't'en pri', ma p'tit' Rose,
> Malgré qu't'es pas bien avec eux.
> Je n'sais rien de c'qui leur arrive. . . .
> Vrai, c'est pas pour fair' du pallas,
> Mais j'voudrais bien qu'moman m'écrive,
>   A Mazas.

Then there is the decrepit old beggar; the "lily-livered" creature (*j'ai les foi's blancs*) who laments his useless cowardice in regard to matters of assault and battery, but is candid enough to think that at all events he will come to no violent end himself:

Ma tête . . . alle aura des ch'veux blancs,

the socialist workman, with his *Faut pus d'tout ça . . . faut pus de rien;* the streetwalker, her lover and her jealousies, the grave-digger, who ends all:

Comm' des marié's, couverts d'fleurs,
Tous les matins on m'en apporte,
Avec leurs parfums, leurs odeurs. . . .
Moi j'trouv' que ça sent bon, la morte.

J'les prends dans mes bras, à mon tour,
Et pis j'les berce. . . . Et pis j'les couche,
En r'inflant la goulé d'amour
Qui s'éshappe encor' de leur bouche.

You may say that these are not agreeable people to be introduced to, and here is a book, certainly, which it is open to everyone not to read. But such people exist in real life, and they are brought before us here, as they so rarely are in the literature which professes to be realistic, with an absolute realism. Bruant's taste lies in the direction of a somewhat *macabre* humour; he gives us, by preference, the darker side of these dark and shadowed lines; but if there is much that he leaves out of the picture, at all events he introduces nothing into it which is not to be found in the reality which it professes to copy. Compare, for instance, *les gueux* of Bruant with those of Richepin. Bruant is a human document, a bit of crude but exact observation; Richepin gives us nothing but impossible rhetoric about impossible persons. And who would not give all the pseudo-philosophy, the pretentious and preposterous pessimism of the writer of *Les Blasphèmes* for this little casual, irresponsible moral, the comment on the end of a nameless soldier who had been guillotined for committing a murder:

> S'i's'rait parti pour el 'Tonquin,
> I's's'rait fait crever l'casaquin
>   Comm' Rivière. . . .
> Un jour on aurait p't'êt' gravé,
> Sur un marbre ou sur un pavé,
>   L'nom d'sa mière.

So resigned, in so desperate a resignation under whatever fate may send, are these

COVER OF 'LE MIRLITON'

[*To face p.* 62.

children of the gutter; philosophers, in their way, since they can accept fortune or misfortune without surprise, if also without thankfulness. Their resignation, their savageries, brutal affections, drunken gaieties, obscene delights; all these Bruant has realised and presented in the two volumes of *Dans la Rue*, which sum up, as nothing else in contemporary literature does, the whole life of the streets, where that life is most typical, curious, and interesting, in Paris, along the dreary sweep of the outer boulevards.

1895.

A BOOK OF FRENCH VERSES

A BOOK OF FRENCH VERSES

Years ago, when I was in Paris, and used to go and see Verlaine every week in his hospital, I remember he burst out suddenly one day into eulogies of Charles Cros, and asked me if I had ever read *Le Coffret de Santal*. On my saying no, he urged me to read it, and began to speak, in his generous way, of what it seemed to him he had learnt from that poet of one book. It was a good while before I succeeded in finding a copy; but at last I got it, and read it, I remember, at that time, with an enchantment which I cannot entirely recapture as I turn over the pages again to-day. Not long afterwards I was at a literary house, and I overheard someone being addressed as Dr. Cros. I asked him if he was related to Charles Cros; his brother, he told me. Finding me enthusiastic, he

talked freely, giving me quite a new idea of
Charles Cros as a man of science, I believe
the discoverer of something or other, as well
as a fantastic poet. Dr. Cros told me that his
brother had left a number of MS. poems, at
his death in 1888; that they were in his own
possession, that he would be glad to publish
them, but that Charles Cros was so little
known that no publisher could be found
to undertake the publication. I promised to
write something about *Le Coffret de Santal*,
but, other things coming in the way, I wrote
nothing. I had almost lost sight of the man
and his book, when, as I was in Paris on my
way back from Spain, I was unexpectedly
reminded of my promise. I was talking with
Yvette Guilbert, whose knowledge of French
literature has often surprised me; but I was
never more surprised than when she said,
à propos of nothing at all: " Why have you
never translated anything from Charles Cros
—you, who have translated so many things
from Verlaine?" "But do you know Charles
Cros?" I said, forgetting to conceal my surprise. "But I adore him," she said, and began

to quote his verses. I promised to translate one of his poems. To-day it occurs to me to keep both my promises.

Well, as I turn out this *Sandal-wood Casket*, full of *bibelots d'emplois incertains*, made out of *sourires, fleurs, baisers, essences*, I seem to find myself at that moment in French literature when the *Parnasse* was becoming not less artificially naïve and perverse at once. It belongs to the period of *Les Amours Jaunes* of Tristan Corbière and the *Rimes de Joie* of Théodore Hannon, both of which you will find praised and defined in Huysmans' *A Rebours*; but it is more genuine, and more genuinely poetical than either. Learning much from Gautier in his form, from Baudelaire for his atmosphere, and, more than from either, from the popular songs of many countries, he seems to anticipate Verlaine in

Des choses absurdes vraiment,

metre and sentiment. And yet he has still the habit of writing in which boats had

Mât de nacre et voile en satin,
Rames d'ivoire.

He seems at times to be accepting every commonplace of poetry, but the commonplaces turn diaphanous under his touch, and come to us with little pallid, pathetic graces, like toys in tears, or as if Dresden China shepherdesses had begun to weep.

> Ma belle amie est morte
> Et voilà qu'on la porte
> En terre, ce matin,
> En souliers de satin.

It is all poetry made up by one who has lived a faint, scarcely passionate, over-dainty life *avec les fleurs, avec les femmes*. You might be deceived into thinking him more real, or more unreal, than he is.

> Ce n'est plus l'heure des tendresses
> Jalouses, ni des faux serments,

but of a kind of remembering tenderness, in which there is something of the senses, something of chaste ideals, and more self-pity than really poignant sorrow. The poem called *Lento*, perhaps the best poem in the volume, is wonderfully touching, as it murmurs almost sobbingly in one's ear, going on to an effect really of slow music, in its delicate, returning cadences. It gives us, in its evasive, whimsically ironical way, a sort of philosophy of just these perfumed sensations which can so easily turn painful or overpowering.

Mais il ne faut pas croire à l'âme des contours,

it cries, with a child's surprise; and it is with a darker, more *macabre* sense of the soiling mystery of death, and the end of beauty, that a poem called *Wasted Words*, which I have translated for a specimen, sums up the attitude of the universe towards woman and of woman towards the universe:—

> After the bath the chambermaid
>   Combs out your hair. The peignoir falls
> In pleated folds. You turn your head
>   To hear the mirror's madrigals.
>
> Does not the mirror's voice remind
>   Your pride: This body, fair in vain,
> Decrepit shelter of a kind
>   Of soul, must find the dust again.
>
> Then shall this delicate flesh forsake
>   The bones it veiled, and worms intrude
> Where all is emptiness, and make
>   A busy nest in solitude.

There, no more white; but brown earth strewn
  Heavily on your bony cheeks.
No gleaming lustres, but the moon.
  These are the words your mirror speaks.

You listen with a soulless smile,
  Too proud to heed the thing they say;
For woman mocks at time, the while
  To-morrow feeds on yesterday.

That is characteristic enough, in its touches of old sentiment and new, in its not unsuccessful aim at effect, in its fantastic modernity; but it is more emphatic than most of these poems, which are indeed at times as sharp and clear as a Latin epigram, but more often vague, floating, really songs, and at times daintily disquieting, little perfumed cries. Perfume is indeed the word that returns oftenest under one's pen as one tries to evoke the actual atmosphere of these pages. The *Sandal-wood Casket* is a cabinet of scents, or contains one, scenting all its other stuffs and trinkets. Baudelaire has taught all modern poets the suggestive value of perfumes, but no one has ever used them with such constant and elaborate felicity. Exotic always, now Chinese, now Ethiopian, now gipsy, now the discord of a night of insomnia, now the penetrating, unreal harmony of a haschisch dream, perfumes steam up out of all these pages; yes, even natural perfumes, out of the hayfields and hedges of the real country. For Charles Cros is not so morbid as one is at first inclined to suppose. Is it really with any sincerity that he says: "Je me tue à vouloir me civiliser l'âme"? And is all this Parisian exoticism really a kind of revenge of nature upon one not naturally, or not exclusively, limited to what is most like the bibelot in humanity? At all events, here, in the midst of these tender, and fantastic, and pathetic sentimentalities, are the delightfully humorous *Grains de Sel*, which one should have heard their writer sing for the full enjoyment of them; the *Hareng Saur*, which has a little immortality of its own, among people hardly aware whom it is by; the *Chanson de Sculpteurs*, which sums up Montmartre; and the *Brave Homme*, which anticipates Aristide Bruant. A set of fifteen *dizains* parodies Coppée, doing his *Annals of the Poor* better than he could do them. It was the time of paradoxes when this book was written; it has indeed always been very French, and in every time very modern, to have irony or humour for a part of one's equipment as a poet; and Charles Cros is very French, and in his own time was very modern.

1899.

Mes mains dans les vôtres

Yvette Guilbert

[*To face p.* 77.

YVETTE GUILBERT

She is tall, thin, a little angular, most winningly and girlishly awkward, as she wanders on to the stage with an air of vague distraction. Her shoulders droop, her arms hang limply. She doubles forward in an automatic bow in response to the thunders of applause, and that curious smile breaks out along her lips and rises and dances in her bright blue eyes, wide open in a sort of child-like astonishment. Her hair, a bright auburn, rises in soft masses above a large pure forehead. She wears a trailing dress, striped yellow and pink, without ornamentation. Her arms are covered with long black gloves. The applause stops suddenly; there is a hush of suspense; she is beginning to sing.

And with the first note you realise the difference between Yvette Guilbert and all the rest of the world. A sonnet by Mr. André Raffalovich states just that difference so subtly that I must quote it to help out my interpretation:—

> If you want hearty laughter, country mirth—
>   Or frantic gestures of an acrobat,
> Heels over head—or floating lace skirts worth
>   I know not what, a large eccentric hat
> And diamonds, the gift of some dull boy—
>   Then when you see her do not wrong Yvette,
> Because Yvette is not a clever toy,
>   A tawdry doll in fairy limelight set.
> And should her song sound cynical and base
>   At first, herself ungainly, or her smile
> Monotonous—wait, listen, watch her face:
>   The sufferings of those the world calls vile
> She sings, and as you watch Yvette Guilbert,
> You too will shiver, seeing their despair.

Now to me Yvette Guilbert was exquisite from the first moment. "Exquisite!" I said under my breath, as I first saw her come upon the stage. She sang *Sainte Galette*, and as I listened to the song I felt a cold shiver run down my back, that *frisson* which no dramatic art, save that of Sarah Bernhardt, had ever given me. I had heard about her, but it was not quite this that I was expecting, so poignant, so human,

that I could scarcely endure the pity of it.
It made me feel that I was wicked; I, to
have looked at these dreadfully serious things
lightly. But it is not by her personal
charm that she thrills you, and I admit
that her personal charm could be called in
question. It must be said, too, that she can
do pure comedy—that she can be merely,
deliciously gay. There is one of her songs
in which she laughs, chuckles, and trills a
rapid flurry of broken words and phrases,
with the sudden, spontaneous, irresponsible
mirth of a bird. But where she is most
herself is in a manner of tragic comedy which
has never been seen on the music-hall stage
from the beginning. It is the profoundly
sad and essentially serious comedy which
one sees in Forain's marvellous designs—
those rapid outlines which, with the turn of
a pencil, give you the whole existence of
those base sections of society which our art
in England is mainly forced to ignore.
People call the art of Forain immoral, they
call Yvette Guilbert's songs immoral. That
is merely the conventional misuse of a conventional word. The art of Yvette Guilbert

is certainly the art of realism. She brings before you the real life drama of the streets, of the pot-house; she shows you the seamy side of life behind the scenes; she calls things by their right names. But there is not a touch of sensuality about her, she is neither contaminated nor contaminating by what she sings; she is simply a great, impersonal, dramatic artist, who sings realism as others write it.

In one of her songs, *Sainte Galette*, she represents a denizen of the Quartier Bréda, praying in her room, at nightfall, to "Our Lady of Cash" — the great omnipotent "Sainte Galette." The verses are really powerful; the music, a sort of dirge or litany, is intensely pathetic. And as Yvette Guilbert sings, in her quiet, thrilling voice, which becomes harsher, for effect, in the lower notes, which becomes a moan, an absolute heart-breaking moan, in that recurrent cry of "Sainte Galette," it is the note of sheer tragedy that she strikes. She literally shook me; she made me shiver; she brought tears to my eyes. In *Je suis pocharde*—where the words are more commonplace—Yvette

YVETTE GUILBERT

Guilbert brings into what might so easily be a merely vulgar representation of a drunken woman something of that tragic savour which gives artistic value as well as moral sanction to her most hazardous assumptions. Her gamut in the purely comic is wide; with an inflection of the voice, a bend of that curious long thin body which seems to be embodied gesture, she can suggest, she can portray, the humour that is dry, ironical, coarse (I will admit), unctuous even. Her voice can be sweet or harsh; it can chirp, lilt, chuckle, stutter; it can moan or laugh, be tipsy or distinguished. Nowhere is she conventional; nowhere does she even resemble any other French singer. Voice, face, gestures, pantomime—all are different, all are purely her own. She is a creature of contrasts, and suggests at once all that is innocent and all that is perverse. She has the pure blue eyes of a child, eyes that are cloudless, that gleam with a wicked ingenuousness, that close in the utter abasement of weariness, that open wide in all the expressionlessness of surprise. Her naïveté is perfect, and perfect, too, is that strange subtle smile of comprehension that closes the period. A great impersonal artist, depending as she does entirely on her expressive power, her dramatic capabilities, her gift for being moved, for rendering the emotions of those in whom we do not look for just that kind of emotion, she affects one all the time as being, after all, removed from what she sings of—an artist whose sympathy is an instinct, a divination. There is something automatic in all fine histrionic genius, and I find some of the charm of the automaton in Yvette Guilbert. The real woman, one fancies, is the slim, bright-haired girl who looks so pleased and so amused when you applaud her, and whom it pleases to please you just because it is amusing. She could not tell you how she happens to be a great artist; how she has found a voice for the tragic comedy of cities; how it is that she makes you cry when she sings of sordid miseries. "That is her secret," we are accustomed to say; and I like to imagine that it is a secret which she herself has never fathomed.

The difference between Yvette Guilbert and

YVETTE GUILBERT

[*To face p.* 84.

every other singer on the variety stage is the
difference between Sarah Bernhardt and every
other actress. There are plenty of women
who sing comic songs with talent: here is a
woman who sings a new tragic variety of
comedy and sings it with genius. The word
"creation" has come to have a casual enough
meaning in regard to any new performance on
the stage, but in this case it is an epithet of
simple justice. This new, subtle, *tourmentée*
way of singing the miseries of the poor and
the vices of the miserable is absolutely a
creation; it brings at once a new order of
subject and a novel manner of presentment
into the comic répertoire, and it lifts the
entertainment of the music-hall into a really
high region of art. To hear her sing six
songs, all quite different in tone—*La Petite
Curieuse*, *La Terre*, Béranger's *Lisette*, *Morphinée*, *Les Demoiselles à Marier*, and *Çà fait
toujours plaisir*—is to realise how wide her
range is. One song, for instance, *La Terre*,
which is serious to the point of solemnity,
and in which the whole effect consists in the
deep feeling and the delicately varied intonation given to the refrain at every recurrence,

gave me much more pleasure than Béranger's *Lisette*, the "grisette de quinze ans." *Morphinée* is sheer tragedy; it is a song by that clever, eccentric, never quite satisfactory person, Jean Lorrain, and it tells all the horror of a life enslaved by morphine. Words and music are singularly apt and mutually expressive, and the rise of the voice, into a sort of dull, yet intense monotony, at the words "je suis hallucinée," is one of the most thrilling effects that even Yvette has ever obtained. The whole thing—sordid, horrible, crazed, as it is—is, as a piece of acting, incomparably expressive, and it is always restrained within the severest artistic limits. *La Petite Curieuse* and *Çà fait toujours plaisir* are more conventional, as songs; slight, neatly done, quite finished in their way, and with some of that perverse naïveté which was, I believe, Yvette Guilbert's earliest discovery in method. *Les Demoiselles à Marier*, the most cynical and subtle of her studies in the young lady of the period, carries this method to a far finer perfection. In what it says and what it suggests it is excessively piquant: really witty, with a distinctively French wit, it has all the fine malice of *Les Demoiselles de Pensionat*, and an even finer, because a more varied, expressiveness. It is in this expressiveness that the secret of Yvette Guilbert lies, and the secret of the expressiveness is, partly, a conscientious attention to detail. Other people are content with making an effect, say, twice in the course of a song. Yvette insists on getting the full meaning out of every line, and, with her, to grasp a meaning is to have found an effect. It is genius, which must be born, not made; and it is also that "infinite capacity for taking pains." I remember her saying to me, "Other women are just as clever as I am, but if I make up my mind that I will do a thing I always do it. I try, and try, and try, until I succeed." There the true artist spoke, and the quality I claim for Yvette Guilbert, above all other qualities, is that she is a true artist, an artist as genuine, and in her own way as great, as any actress on any stage.

1900.

DANCERS AND DANCING

La Mélinite
(Moulin Rouge)

Olivier Metra's Waltz of Roses
  Sheds in a rhythmic shower
  The very petals of the flowers;
And all to roses,
  The rouge of petals in a shower.

Down the long hall the dance returning
  Rounds the full circle, rounds
  The perfect rose of lights and sounds,
The rose returning
  Into the circle of its rounds.

Alone, apart, one dancer watches
  Her mirrored, morbid grace;
  Before the mirror, face to face,
Alone she watches
  Her morbid, vague, ambiguous grace.

Before the mirror's dance of shadows
  She dances in a dream,
  And she and they together seem
A dance of shadows,
  Alike the shadows of a dream.

The orange-rosy lamps are trembling
  Between the lamps that turn;
  In ruddy flowers of flame that burn
The lights are trembling:
  The shadows and the dancers turn.

And, enigmatically smiling,
  In the mysterious night,
  She dances for her own delight,
A shadow smiling
  Back to a shadow in the night.

DANCERS AND DANCING

I

It was in May, 1892, that, having crossed the streets of Paris from the hotel where I was staying, the Hôtel Corneille, in the Latin Quarter (made famous by Balzac in his superb story, *Z. Marcas*), I found myself in Le Jardin de Paris, where I saw for the first time La Mélinite. She danced in a quadrille: young and girlish, the more provocative because she played as a prude, with an assumed modesty; *décolletée* nearly to the waist, in the Oriental fashion. She had long black curls around her face; and had about her a depraved virginity.

And she caused in me, even then, a curious sense of depravity that perhaps comes into the verses I wrote on her. There, certainly, on the night of May 22nd, danced in her feverish, her perverse, her enigmatical beauty, La Mélinite, to her own image in the mirror:

A shadow smiling
Back to a shadow in the night

as she cadenced Olivier Métra's *Valse des Roses*.

The *chahut*, which she danced, is the successor, one might almost say the renaissance, of the *cancan*. Roughly speaking, the *cancan* died with the Bal Mabille, the *chahut* was born with the Jardin de Paris. The effervescent Bal Bullier of the Quartier Latin, in its change from the Closerie des Lilas, of the days of Murger, may be said to have kept the tradition of the thing, and, with the joyous and dilapidated Moulin de la Galette of the heights of Montmartre, to have led the way in the establishment of the present school of dancing. But it was at the Jardin de Paris, about the year 1884, that the *chahut*, or the *quadrille naturaliste*, made its appearance, and, with La Goulue and Grille-d'Égout, came to stay. The dance is simply a quadrille in delirium—a quadrille in which the steps are punctuated by *le port d'armes* (or high kicks), with *le grand écart* (or "the splits") for parenthesis. *Le port d'armes* is done by standing on one foot and holding the other upright in the air; *le grand écart* by sitting on the floor with the legs absolutely horizontal. Beyond these two fundamental rules of the game, everything almost is left to the fantasy of the performer, and the fantasy of the whirling people of the Moulin Rouge, the Casino, the Jardin de Paris, the Elysée Montmartre, is free, fertile, and peculiar. Even in Paris you must be somewhat ultra-modern to appreciate it, and to join, night after night, those avid circles which form so rapidly, here and there on the ball-room floor, as a waltz-rhythm ends, and a placard bearing the word "Quadrille" is hung out from the musicians' gallery.

Of all the stars of the *chahut*, the most charming, the most pleasing, is La Goulue. Still young, though she has been a choreographic celebrity for seven or eight years; still fresh, a veritable "queen of curds and cream" among the too white and the too red women of the Moulin Rouge; she has that simple, ingenuous air which is, perhaps, the last refinement, to the perverse, of perversity. To dance the *chahut*, to dance it with infinite excitement, and to look like a milkmaid: that, surely, is a triumph of natural genius! Grille-

d'Égout, her companion and rival, is not so
interesting. She is dark, serious, correct, perfectly accomplished in her art, and a professor
of it, but she has not the high spirits, the
entrain, the attractiveness, of La Goulue. In
Nini-Patte-en-l'Air, a later, though an older,
leader of the *quadrille naturaliste*, and, like
Grille-d'Égout, a teacher of eccentric dancing,
we find, perhaps, the most typical representa-
tive of the *chahut* of to-day. She is not young,
she is not pretty, she is thin, short of stature,
dark, with heavy eyebrows, coarse, irregular
features. Her face is worn and haggard,
almost ghastly; her mouth is drawn into an
acute, ambiguous, ironical smile; her roving
eyes have a curious, intent glitter. She has
none of the *gaminerie* of La Goulue: hers is
a severely self-conscious art, and all her extravagances are perfectly deliberate. But with
what mastery they are done, with what tireless
agility, what tireless ingenuity in invention!
Always cold, collected, "the Maenad of the
Decadence," it is with a sort of "learned fury"
that she dances; and she has a particular trick
—the origin of her nickname—a particular
quiver of the foot as the leg is held rigid in

the air — which is her sign and signature.
After these three distinguished people come
many. There is La Mélinite, Rayon d'Or, La
Sauterelle, Etoile Filante, and many another;
of whom La Mélinite is certainly the most
interesting. She is tall, slim, boyish in figure,
décolletée in the Eastern fashion, in a long slit;
she dances with a dreamy absorption, a conventional air, as of perverted sanctity, remote,
ambiguous. And then there is La Macarona
of the Elysée-Montmartre, whose sole title to
distinction lies in the extraordinary effrontery
of her costume.

II

On my way to Nini-Patte-en-l'Air's I
stopped at a second-hand bookstall, where
I purchased a particular edition which I had
long been seeking, of a certain edifying work
of great repute. Opening the book at random,
I found myself at Chapter XX, *De Amore
Solitudinis et Silenti*. "Relinque curiosa," I
read. Then I put the book in my pocket and
went on to Nini-Patte-en-l'Air's.

Of course, I had been at the Trafalgar

Square Theatre—two Saturdays ago, was it not?—when the unaccountable British public had applauded so frankly and so vigorously its first glimpse of a *quadrille naturaliste* in England. But now I was going, in response to a special invitation from Madame Nini, to see what I fancied would interest me far more, a private lesson in the art of the *chahut*. I found the hotel, but not, at first, the front door. In the bar no one knew of a front door, but I might go upstairs, they said, if I liked: that way, through the door on the right. I went upstairs, found a waiter, and presently Nini-Patte-en-l'Air bustled into the room, and told me to make myself quite at home. Nini is charming, with her intense nervous vivacity, her quaint seriousness, her little professional airs; befitting the directress of the sole *école du chahut* at present existing in the world. We have all seen her on the stage, and the little, plain, thick-set woman with the vivid eyes and the enigmatic mouth, is just the same on the stage and off. She is the same because she has an individuality of her own, which gives her, in her own kind of dancing, a place apart—an individuality which is reinforced by a degree of accomplishment to which neither La Goulue nor Grille-d'Égout, neither La Sauterelle nor Rayon-d'Or, can for a moment pretend. And I found that she takes herself very seriously; that she is justly proud of being the only *chahut* dancer who has made an art out of a caprice, as well as the only one who has conquered all the difficulties of her own making, the only executant at once faultless and brilliant. We talked of many thing, I of Paris and she of London, for which she professes an immense enthusiasm; then she told me of her triumphant tour in America, and how she conquered America by the subtle discretion of her *dessous*, which were black. Blue, pink, yellow, white, she experimented with all colours; but the American standpoint was only precisely found and flattered by the factitious reserve of black. Then, as she explained to me all the technique of her art, she would jump up from the armchair in which she was sitting, shoot a sudden leg, surprisingly, into the air, and do the *grand écart* on the hearthrug. But the pupils? Oh, the pupils were coming; and Madame and I had just finished moving the heavy oak table into a corner, when the door opened, and they came in.

I was introduced, firstly, to La Ténébreuse, a big woman of long experience, whom I found to be more supple than her figure indicated. Églantine came next, a tall, strong, handsome, dignified-looking girl, with dark eyes and eyebrows; she is in her second year, and has been with Nini in America. Then came Épi-d'Or, a timid, yet gay, rather English little blonde, who makes her *début* in London. They sat down meekly, like good little school-girls, and each came forward as she was called, went through her exercises, and returned to her seat by the door. And those exercises! It was not a large room, and when a tall girl lay at full length on the floor, and Nini bent over her, seized one of her legs, and worked it about as if it were a piece of india-rubber, the space seemed quite sufficiently occupied. When Églantine took her third step towards me, kicking her hand on the level of her eyes at each step, I tried to push back my chair a little closer to the wall, in case of accidents; and the big girl, La Ténébreuse, when she did the *culbute*, or somersault, ending with the *grand écart*, or the splits, finished at, almost on, my feet. I saw the preparatory exercises, *le brisement*, or dislocation, and *la série*, or the high-kick, done by two in concert; and then the different poses of the actual dance itself: *la guitare*, in which the leg is held almost at right angles with the body, the ankle supported by one hand; *le port d'armes*, in which the leg is held upright, one hand clasping the heel of the boot—a position of great difficulty, on which *le salut militaire* is a slight variation; *la Jambe derrière la tête*, a position which requires the most elaborate acrobatic training, and which is perhaps as painful to see as it must be to do; *le croisement*, which ends a figure and is done by two or four dancers, forming a sort of cross-pattern by holding their heels together in the air, on a level with the eyes; and *le grand écart*, or the splits, which is done either by gliding gradually out (the usual method), or by a sudden jump in which the split is done in the air, and the body falls violently to the ground, like a pair of compasses which have opened out by their own weight. It was all very instructive, very curious, very amusing.

"Relinque curiosa," said the book in my pocket. But I was far from being in that monastic mood as I watched these extraordinary contortions, done so blithely, yet so seriously, by Ténébreuse, Églantine, and Épi-d'Or; Nini-Patte-en-l'Air giving her orders with that professional air now more fixed than ever on her attentive face. It was all so discreet, after a fashion, in its methodical order; so comically indiscreet, in another sense. I am avid of impressions and sensations; and here, certainly, was a new sensation, an impression of something not easily to be seen elsewhere. I sat and pondered, my chair pushed close back to the wall, Nini-Patte-en-l'Air by my side, and before me Ténébreuse, Églantine, and Épi-d'Or.

1897.

LEON BLOY: THE THANKLESS BEGGAR

LEON BLOY: THE THANKLESS BEGGAR

THE writer whom Octave Mirabeau has called *le plus somptueux écrivain de notre temps*, of whom Remy de Gourmont has said that he is *un de plus grands créateurs d'images que la terre ait portés*, is indeed "himself remarkable." In *Le Mendiant Ingrat*, a journal kept during the years 1892–1895, which forms a sort of autobiography, he writes: "J'ai vécu, sans vergogne, dans une extrême solitude, peuplée des ressentiments et des désirs fauves que mon exécration des contemporains enfantait, écrivant ou vociférant ce qui me paraissait juste." "Écrivant ou vociférant," for the writing of this strange pamphleteer of genius is at times an almost inarticulate cry of rage or of disgust. "Je suis l'enclume au fond du gouffre," he cries, in a letter to Henry de Groux, written at a time when his wife, believed to be at the point of death, had received extreme unction, "l'enclume de Dieu, qui me fait souffrir ainsi parce qu'il m'aime, je le sais bien. L'enclume de Dieu, au fond du gouffre! Soit. C'est une bonne place pour retentir vers Lui." In the dedication of his new book he invites a friend to make his escape "des Lieux Communs où l'on dîne pour venir héroïquement ronger avec moi des crânes d'imbéciles dans la solitude." It is a dish on which he has sharpened his teeth all his life, and his hunger is deadly. Bloy tells us that he lives entirely on alms, and he affirms that it is the duty of man toward man, and especially of Christian toward Christian, to supply the need of one whose poverty is honourable. "Pourquoi voudrait-on que je ne m'honorasse pas d'avoir été un mendiant, et, surtout, un 'mendiant ingrat'?" His journal is the journal of Lazarus at the gate, lifting up his voice against the rich man who has thrown him the crumbs from his table. Here is no anarchism, no political or social grievance; it is the outcry of a Catholic and an aristocrat of letters, unable to "make his way in the world," because he will not "prostitute himself" to any servile or lying tasks. Has a man the right to claim his right to live, and to claim it without shame, and without gratitude to the giver for more than the spirit of the gift? That is the problem which Bloy sets before us. Bloy is a fervent Catholic, he believes in God, he believes that the promises of the Bible are to be taken literally, and that, literally, "the Lord will provide" for his servants. Man, in almsgiving, is but the instrument, often the unwilling instrument, of God; Bloy is therefore ready to receive help from his enemies and to bastinade his friends, in perfect good faith. "I recognise a friend," he says simply, "by his giving me money." He is the living statement of the dependence of man on man, that is, of man on God, who can act only through man. Where he is alone is in his pride in that humiliation of himself, and in his insistence on the duty of others to give him what he is in need of. The most eloquent of his pleadings against the world's commonplaces is No. CXLIV, *Avoir du pain sur la planche. Quand il n'y en a que quelques miettes*, he says, *ça se mange encore. Quand il y en a trop, ça ne se mange pas du tout, ça devient des pierres et c'est avec le pain sur la planche des bourgeois de Jérusalem que fut lapidé le protomartyr.*

But it is not merely in his quality of man and of Christian that Bloy demands alms, it is as the prophet and familiar friend of God. I do not doubt Bloy's sincerity in believing that he has a "message" to the world. His message, he tells us, is *de notifier la gloire de Dieu*, and it is to notify the glory of God by spoiling the Egyptians, scourging the money-changers out of the Temple, and otherwise helping to cleanse the gutters of creation. It is his mission to be a scavenger, and to spare the cesspool of a friend who might be useful, or the dunghill of an employer who has been useful, materially, would be an act almost criminal. With this conviction in his soul, with a flaming and devouring temperament which must prey on something if it is not to prey mortally on itself, it is not unnatural that he has never been able to "write for money." The artist may indeed write for money, with only comparative harm to himself or to his art. He permits himself to do something which he accounts of secondary importance. But the prophet, who is a voice, must always cry his message; to change a syllable of his message is to sin the unpardonable sin. With him whatever is not absolute truth, truth to conviction, is a wilful lie.

Bloy's *Exégése des Lieux Communs* is a crucifixion of the bourgeois on a cross of the bourgeois' own making. Now it is to the bourgeois, after all, that Bloy appeals for alms, and it is from the bourgeois that he receives it, as he declares (and, indeed, proves) "thanklessly." I am not sure that the conventional estimation of gratitude as one of the main virtues, of gratitude in all circumstances and for all favours received, has not a profoundly bourgeois origin. I have never been able clearly to recognise the necessity, or even the possibility, of gratitude towards anyone for whom I have not a feeling of personal affection, quite apart from any exchange of benefits. The conferring what is called a favour, materially, and the prompt return of a delicate sentiment, gratitude, seems to me a kind of commercialism of the mind, a mere business transaction, in which an honest ex-

change is not always either possible or needful.
The demand for gratitude in return for a gift
comes largely from the respect which most
people have for money; from the idea that
money is the most "serious" thing in the
world, instead of an accident, a compromise,
the symbol of a physical necessity, but a thing
having no real existence in itself, no real importance to the mind which refuses to realise
its existence. Only the miser really possesses
it in itself, in any significant way; for the
miser is an idealist, the poet of gold. To all
others it is a kind of mathematics, and a
synonym for being "respected." You may
say it is necessary, almost as necessary as
breathing, and I will not deny it. Only I
will deny that anyone can be actively grateful
for the power of breathing. He cannot conceive of himself without that power. To
conceive of oneself without money, that is to
say without the means of going on living, is
at once to conceive of the right, the mere
human right, to assistance. If, in addition
to that mere human right, one is convinced
that one is a man of genius, the right becomes
more plainly evident, and if, in addition, one

has a divine "message" for the world, what further need be said? That, I take it, is the argument of Bloy's conviction. It is a problem which I should like to set before Tolstoi. I am not sure that the meekest and the most arrogant enemy of our civilisation would not join hands, Tolstoi's with a gift in it, offered freely and humbly, which Bloy's would take, freely and proudly.

1902.

VICTOR HUGO AND WORDS

VICTOR HUGO AND WORDS

The centenary of Hugo gives this collection a special interest as the last thing from the hand of the master whose astonishing literary career began in 1816. On one of the pages of the *Post-scriptum de ma Vie* he writes: *Mais les fondateurs de religions ont erré, l'analogie n'est pas toujours la logique.* The whole of this book is a vast exercise in analogies. It comes to us as with the voice of a new revelation; it neither proves nor denies, nor does it even argue; from beginning to end it affirms. And the affirmations range over the universe. *L'intelligence est l'épouse, l'imagination est la maîtresse, la mémoire est la servante.* There, on the side of a witty common sense, is one affirmation. Here, in the language of an apocalyptic mysticism, is another: *Et c'est toujours de l'immanent, toujours present, toujours tangible, toujours inexplicable, toujours inconcevable, toujours incontestable, que sort l'agenouillement humain.* There are 270 pages of the most eloquent images in the world—images which seem to bubble out of the brain like uninhabitable worlds out of the creating hands of a mad deity. Every image detaches itself gaily, floats away with supreme confidence into space; and perhaps arrives somewhere: certainly it soon becomes invisible. Monmouth and Macedon are at one for ever in these astonishing pages; every desire of the heart seems to fulfil itself by its mere utterance; there is no longer a truism: A B C have become miraculous again, as they were in the beginning. *Qu'est-ce que l'océan? C'est une permission.* When the ocean is a permission, birds may fly where they please. And these little, hard, sharp sentences are scattered violently in all directions; they rise like fireworks, they fall like comets, lighting up patches of impenetrable darkness. They succeed one another so rapidly that the eyes can scarcely follow them; and each leaves behind it the same blackness.

When Victor Hugo thought that he was

thinking, he was really listening to the inarticulate murmur that words make among themselves as they await the compelling hand of their master. He was master of them all, and they adored him, and they served him so willingly and so swiftly that he never needed to pause and choose among them, or think twice on what errand he should send them. They had started on their errand before he had finished the message he had to give them.

> Par le ciel, dont la mort est le noir machiniste,
> Le sage sur le sort s'accoude, calme et triste,
> Content d'un peu de pain et d'une goutte d'eau,
> Et, pensif, il attend le lever du rideau.

Is not this epigram rather than poetry, ingenuity rather than imagination? Does it not show, in the words of M. de Régnier, a little of *le gigantesque effort du prosateur qui boite d'une antithèse fatigante*? Or take this line,

> La vie est un torchon orné d'une dentelle,

which it has seemed worth giving by itself among the *Tas de Pierres*, a line certainly characteristic of Hugo: can one accept it as a line of poetry, or is it not rather, like the whole passage which we have quoted, an effort of mere prose logic? Poem follows poem, sonorous, ingenious, exterior, made for the most part out of a commonplace which puffs itself out to vast size. They are like clusters of glittering images round the faint light of a tiny idea. One cannot read them without admiration for their astonishing cleverness; still one cannot feel anything but cold admiration, without either interest or sympathy. They are the mathematical piling up of a given structure, in a given way, always the same. Poem repeats poem like an echo; always the same admirable form, finished to a kind of hard clear surface, off which the mind slips, without penetrating it. It is really difficult to read a poem like *Soir d'Avril*, for instance, with its facile forty-five stanzas, so apt, so eloquent, so elegant, so generalised, in which so many pretty things are said about love, but in which love never speaks with its own voice. All these resonant poems about Babel, and hell, and *le grand Etre* contain splendid images, and rise into a fine oratory; but they come to us like the voice of a crowd, not the voice of a man.

Among the fragments in these pages are some epigrams of a Latin sharpness and savour. Take this one, *A un Critique*:—

Un aveugle a le tact très fin, très net, très clair;
Autant que le renard des bois, il a le flair;
Autant que le chamois des monts, il a l'ouïe;
Sa sensibilité, rare, exquise, inouïe,
Du moindre vent coulis lui fait un coup de poing;
Son oreille est subtile et délicate au point
Que lorsque un oiseau chante, il croit qu'un taureau
 beugle.
Quel flair! quel tact! quel goût!—Oui, mais il est
 aveugle.

There, in that merely logical development of an idea, in that strictly calculated progression, you will find the method which really lies hidden in most of the more eloquent, the more obviously poetical, passages in this volume. A poem which impresses by its largeness and loftiness, *Du Haut des Montagnes*, is poetical, if one looks into it, only in its choice of detail; the "mental cartooning" is inadequate, mechanical. It begins:—

Voici les Apennins, les Alpes et les Andes.
Tais-toi, passant, devant ces visions si grandes.
Silence, homme! histrion! Les monts contemplent
 Dieu.

Then comes a powerful and vivid statement of

> Le drame formidable et sombre de l'abîme,
> L'entrée et la sortie étrange de la nuit,

of which the mountains are the spectators; then the reflection:—

> Pour eux, l'homme n'est pas, un peuple s'évapore;

finally, a geographical conclusion:—

> Balkan, sans voir Stamboul, chante son noir salem;
> Sina voit l'infini, mais non Jérusalem.

Is there not in all this something a little obvious, a little made up? Is it not an effect of rhetoric rather than an authentic vision? That the authentic vision can be found in Hugo when Hugo is his finest self, we all know; but in how much of his work, as in the whole, or almost the whole, of this last volume of it, we find that fundamentally insincere rhetoric which is none the less insincere because it is thundered from the hilltop!

The testament of Victor Hugo, *Post-scriptum de ma Vie*, is after all not the last publication of a writer whose energy seems to survive death. Here is *Dernière Gerbe*, the last sheaf, a collection of poems, of which

VICTOR HUGO AND WORDS 121

the earliest dates from 1829. For the most part the poems are complete, but there is a small collection of fragments, called *Tas de Pierres*, single lines, couplets and stanzas; and at the end of the volume are some disconnected scenes and speeches from one or two unfinished plays, *Une Aventure de Don César*, *Maglia*, *Gavoulagoule*.

The poems contained in this volume are all characteristic of Hugo, but not characteristic of Hugo at his best. Take, for example, *Le Rideau*:—

Ce monde, fête ou deuil, palais ou galetas,
Est chimérique, faux, ondoyant, plein d'un tas
De spectres vains, qu'on nomme Amour, Orgueil, Envie.
L'immense ciel bleu pend, tiré sur l'autre vie.
Le vrai drame, où déjà nos coeurs sont rattachés,
Les personnages, vrais, hélas ! nous sont cachés.

It did not matter; there were always more words, and more and more, ready to do his bidding. Listen :—

Pourquoi Virgile est-il inférieur à Homere?
Pourquoi Anacréon est-il inférieur à Pindare?
Pourquoi Ménandre est-il inférieur à Aristophane? Pourquoi Sophocle est-il inférieur à

Eschyle? Pourquoi Lysippe est-il inférieur à Phidias? Pourquoi David est-il inférieur à Isaie? Pourquoi Thucydide est-il inférieur à Herodote? Pourquoi Cicéron est-il inférieur à Démosthene?

There are eight more similar queries, and there the series ends, but there is no reason why it should ever have ended.

"The primitive and myth-making character of his imagination," says Mr. Havelock Ellis, "the tendency to regard metaphors as real, and to accept them as the basis of his mental constructions and doctrines, these tendencies, which Hugo shared with the savage, are dependent on rudimentary emotions and a high degree of ignorance regarding the precise relationship of things."

Which he shared with the savage, yes, with that primitive being which is at the root of every great poet. The poet who is also a philosopher loses nothing as a poet; he adds meaning to beauty. But there is also the poet to whom the vast joy of making is sufficient, who has no curiosity concerning the work of his hands; who makes beauty, and leaves it to others to explain it. "Le beau, c'est la forme," declares Hugo. "La forme est essentielle et absolue; elle vient des entrailles mêmes de l'idée." To work, with Hugo, was almost an automatic process; an enormous somnambulism carried his soul about the world of imagination. Read the *Promontorium Somnii* in this testament; it is a picture in fifty pages, and each sentence is a separate picture. Ideas? ideas come and go, drift away and return; visible and audible ideas helping to make the colours of the picture.

There is beauty in this book, as in everything that Hugo wrote; there is the great poetic orator's mastery of language. Hugo's poetry was never made to be "overheard"; his prose knocks hard at the ear for instant hearing. Even when he dreams, he dreams oratorically; he would have you realise that he is asleep on Patmos. He has strange glimpses. *Le spectre blanc coud des manches à son suaire et devient Pierrot. Quant à la quantité de comédie qui peut se mêler au rêve, qui ne l'a éprouvé? On rit endormi.*

Little passing thoughts, each an analogy, leap out: *L'écho est la rime de la nature. Ce qui fait que la musique plaît tant au commun des hommes, c'est que c'est de la rêverie toute faite.*

Every sentence contains an antithesis or forms an epigram. All is clamour, clangour, and the voice of "loud uplifted angel-trumpets." When it is ended, and one looks back, it is as if one tried to recall the shapes and colours of an avalanche of clouds seen by night over a wide and tossing sea.

1902.

A TRAGIC COMEDY

GEORGE SAND

Madame,

Je prends la liberté de vous envoyer quelques vers que je viens d'écrire en relisant un chapitre d'Indiana; celui où Noun reçoit Raimond dans la chambre de sa maîtresse. Leur peu de valeur ne m'aurait fait hésiter à les mettre sous vos yeux, s'ils n'étaient pour moi une occasion de vous exprimer le sentiment d'admiration sincère et profonde qui les a inspirés.

Agréez, Madame, l'assurance de mon respect —

Alf^d de Musset

[*To face p.* 127.

A TRAGIC COMEDY

In one of the letters now published in their complete form for the first time, Alfred de Musset writes:—"La postérité répétera nos noms comme ceux de ces amants immortels qui n'en ont plus qu'un a eux deux, comme Roméo et Juliette, comme Héloise et Abélard. On ne parlera jamais de l'un sans parler de l'autre." It is true that the name of George Sand instinctively calls up the name of Alfred de Musset, and that his name instinctively calls up hers. But does posterity really repeat the names of "the lovers of Venice" in the same spirit as it repeats the names of the lovers of Verona, or even as it repeats the name of "the learned nun" and her lover? A third name asks to be admitted into the company; posterity queries, "And Pagello?"

This is a question on which the last word will probably never be said; but the most important documents in the case, certainly, are those which have now been published in as entire a condition as George Sand's careful scissors left them. They were preserved by her, it is clear, as a justification of herself; and there is no doubt that they justified her in her own eyes. It is still possible to read them through, and, while admitting the troubles that she had to suffer from a spoilt child like Musset, to sympathise, if not actually to take sides, with Musset rather than with her. Musset's letters, with all their extravagance, sentimentality, literary affectations, petulances, fits and starts of feeling, hysteria even, are the letters of a man who is really in love, who really suffers acutely. George Sand's letters are maternal, affectionate, reasonable, soothing, at times worried into a little energy of feeling; but they are the letters of a woman who has never really loved the man whom she has left for another. "Tu as vingt-trois ans, et voilà que j'en ai trente-et-un," she says, in one of the last of them; and there, certainly, is the explanation of much. In one of the first letters after Musset's flight from Venice, he writes to her:

"Tu t'étais trompée; tu t'es crue ma maîtresse, tu n'étais que ma mère;" and she answers, "Peu importe!" She calls him "Mon petit frère, mon enfant," and cries, "Ah! qui te soignera et qui soignerai-je? Qui aura besoin de moi et de qui voudrai-je prendre soin désormais?" The real woman speaks there, and, coming when it does in the story, it is not the word of a lover. It expresses the need of an organisation, the *besoin de nourrir cette maternelle sollicitude qui s'est habituée à veiller sur un être souffrant et fatigué*. Between this instinct of compassion and the impulse of love there is a great gulf. It is an instinct that may be heroism in a woman who renounces love for its sake. But a very harsh kind of comedy steps in when the woman writes of her present lover to her former lover: "Je l'aimais comme un père, et tu étais notre enfant à tous deux."

It is true that Musset, genuine as his letters seem to be in their expression of a real feeling, is not always absorbed in it to the exclusion of other interests. A month after he has left Venice, in the midst of a troubled and very serious letter, he says suddenly:—

Je m'en vais faire un roman. J'ai bien envie d'écrire notre histoire : il me semble que cela me guérirait et m'élèverait le cœur.

He asks her permission which she gives readily; she is writing something else, not about herself or him at all, a part of her undeviating course of work, which flows onward, then and always, without change of direction, or in any direction. While he reads *Werther* and meditates the *Confession d'un Enfant du Siècle*, a book certainly made out of the best of his heart and the most honest part of his senses, she is asking him to correct her proofs for the *Revue des Deux Mondes*, and to insert the chapter-divisions, which she is afraid in her haste she has forgotten. Later in the book the letters become more exciting. They meet again, and Musset forgets everything but his love. The letter from Baden is an outcry almost of agony. The words gasp and rush: *Je suis perdu, vois-tu, je suis noyé, inondé d'amour; je ne sais plus si je vis, si je mange, si je marche, si je respire, si je parle; je sais que j'aime. Je t'aime, ma chair.* Pagello is no longer between them, but there is something, as before, between them; she tries to love him again, seems about to succeed, and then there is the new, inevitable parting with which these letters end. In some of the brief last letters she, too, seems to suffer, and the distressing reasonableness of tone gives way to a less guarded emphasis. But she recovers herself, and with the cry of *Mes enfans, mes enfans!* leaves him.

Such value as the episode may have had to the rarer genius of the two is to be found, perhaps, in the phrase of Musset, true most likely: *Sois fière, mon grand et brave George, tu as fait un homme d'un enfant.* The amount of "self-improvement" derived by George Sand from the same experience is a more negligible quantity. Musset at least was to write a few songs and a few comedies which were worth any "expense of spirit" whatever; and if George Sand helped to make him the man who was capable of writing these, she did well. Her own sentimental education could probably have done without Musset easily enough; we might have had one *Elle et Lui* the less, but we should have had one *Lucrezia Floriani* the more. Musset or Pagello, Chopin or Pierre Leroux, it mattered little to her; each added an appreciable interest to her life, and an appreciable volume or so to her work. But of no man could it be said that he had been needful to her, that he had helped to make her what she was. She went through life taking what she wanted, and she ended her days in calm self-content, the most famous of contemporary women. It is possible that in the future she will be remembered chiefly as the friend or enemy of some of the greatest men of her time.

1904.

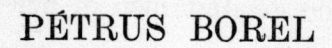

PÉTRUS BOREL

PÉTRUS BOREL

[*To face p.* 135.

PÉTRUS BOREL

The name of Pétrus Borel has come to be a laughing-stock to the Philistine, a byword to the Bourgeois. His nickname, "le lycanthrope," is remembered, but it is forgotten that it was of his own christening. What Gautier said of him as a friend, and Baudelaire as a critic; all that and the fact that he was the chief of a cénacle and "un roi qui s'en allait," all but a few seekers after lost reputations have forgotten. He is a figure fantastic but not grotesque, a defier of order but a slave of letters. He dreamed of conquering the world. He was a dandy, whether with a "gilet à la Robespierre" or naked under a tiger-skin. His whole work, scattered in reviews and journals, and never reprinted, is contained in a novel, a book of short stories, and a book of verse. None of them are accessible, and one, not the least remarkable, exists only in its original edition of 1833, of which I have a copy. No one has ever yet done them entire justice.

Pierre-Joseph Borel de Hauterive was born in Lyons 26 June, 1809, and died at Mostaganem, in Algeria, on 14 July, 1859. The events of his life are of no great importance, but his ill-luck was continuous. He was set to be an architect, and built a few houses and the once famous Cirque of the Boulevard du Temple. But he preferred the studios of his friends, and was soon penniless. His books brought him no money, he founded newspapers with names such as *Le Satan*, *L'âne d'or*, and wrote articles, stories and poems wherever he could get them taken; finally, in 1846, through the help of Gautier and Mme. de Giradin, was appointed Inspector of Colonies at Mostaganem. There he built a house for himself which he called "Haute Pensée." In 1848 he was turned out of his post, and afterwards removed to another. He married, and had a son, Aldéran-André-Pétrus-Benoni; and died in misery in the year 1859.

The *jeune et fatal poète* has described himself under an imaginary name in the preface of one of his books: its exactitude is confirmed by all the portraits painted and the eulogies written by his friends. The two mottoes on the title-page of *Rapsodies* render its character with great exactness. One is chosen from Régnier, one from Malherbe. The former affirms the author to be,

Hautain, audacieux, conseiller de lui-même,
Et d'un coeur obstiné se heurte à ce qu'il aime.

The second, in the name of the book, declares:

Vous, dont les censures s'étendent
Dessus les ouvrages de tous,
Ce livre se moque de vous.

Nothing more remained to be said, only there is a long preface: the end is fine irony: "Heureusement que pour se consoler de tout cela, il nous reste l'adultère! le tabac de Maryland! et du papel espagnol pour cigaritos." He names himself "Un loup-cervier." "Mon republicanisme, c'est de la lycanthropie!" The word caught, he recaptured it, and "le lycanthrope" will be found among his titles for himself. The book begins and ends with an avowal of poverty, and between that beginning and ending what romantic dreams,—what towers, châtelaines, what satisfaction to have only "a tattered cloak, a poignard, and the skies," if one can also "taste one's sorrows in an elegant tea-cup." The sombre Carlovingian manner is there. Is it from Hugo already that the romantic properties find their way into these pages, and this sort of antithesis:

> Enfer! si ta peine est ma peine,
> Qu'en ce moment tu dois souffrir!

It was in the air, and all the gay and fierce love-songs were what everybody was writing. What is personal comes in, here for instance, where the vagabond life of Pétrus and his companions is indicated in a single quaint stanza:

> Chats de coulisse, endévés!
> Devant la salle ébahie
> Traversant, rideaux levés,
> Le Théâtre de la vie.

And there is the ceaseless refrain which returns throughout his whole work:

> Naître, souffrir, mourir, c'est tout dans la nature
> Ce que l'homme perçoit; car elle est un bouquin
> Qu'on ne peut déchiffrer : un manuscrit arabe
> Aux mains d'un muletier : hors le titre et le fin
> Il n'interprète rien, rien, pas une syllable.

The wolf barks harshly enough, and to little purpose, in the political pieces, but has not yet tasted blood. *Champavert* is hardly anticipated in *Agarite*, the one dainty fragment of dialogue, with its instant of drama. All this, however, is in the interval, and we end with a desperate epilogue: "J'ai faim."

It is curious how many things which Pétrus Borel could not achieve he left as an impetus to others. Few readers probably have paid any heed to the motto of the fifth *Ariette oubliée* of the *Romances sans Paroles*:

> Son joyeux, importun d'un clavecin sonore.

Verlaine's poem is a miraculous transposition of what Borel only suggests in his poem, which is called *Doléance* and is a personal lament. But he has taken from it all that he needs; there is, besides the line quoted, the "Parle, que me veux-tu?" which may be discerned in "Que voudrais-tu de moi?" May not "une main frêle" come from:

Indiscret, d'ou viens tu ? Sans doute une main
  blanche,
 Un beau doigt prisonnier
Dans de riches joyaux a frappé sur ton anche
 D'ivoire et d'ébenier ?

Of a bitter, personal lament, in which the "clavecin sonore" is a mere starting-point, Verlaine has made a floating, vague, and divine dream of music scarcely heard in a twilight: no more than that, but a masterpiece. But to him, as to others, it was Pétrus who had given the first impulse.

Pétrus Borel's best poem is not to be found in the *Rapsodies*, but in the form of a prologue to *Madame Putiphar*. It is filled with a grave and remote phantasy, and in its cold ardour, its romantic equipment, and its naked self under that cloak, it anticipates Baudelaire, and is almost worthy of him. Baudelaire was conscious of its merit, and has defined it as, "un étrange poème, d'une sonorité si éclatante et d'une couleur presque primitive à force d'intensité." The poem is a cavalcade of three adversaries in the soul: the world, a mystic's solitude, and death. The picture of each is given: the first, young, gay in his steel corslet on his caparisoned horse; the second bestrides a bony mule; the third, a hideous gnome, bears at his side a great fishhook, on which hangs nets of unclean creatures. And so, he ends, after praising and cursing each in turn, with admiration and hate.

Ainsi, depuis long-temps, s'entrechoque et se taille
Cet infernal trio,—ces trois fiers spadassins:
Ils ont pris, les méchants, pour leur champ de bataille,
Mon pauvre coeur, meurtri sous leurs coups assassins,
Mon pauvre coeur navré, qui s'affaisse et se broie,
Douteur, religieux, fou, mondain, mécréant!
Quand finira la lutte, et qui m'aura pour proie,—
Dieu le sait!—du Désert, du Monde ou du Néant?

In the year 1833 a book of between four and five hundred pages was published in Paris by the firm of Eugène Renduel, under the title: *Champavert. Contes Immoraux, par Pétrus Borel, le Lycanthrope.* The first thirty-eight pages contain a *Notice sur Champavert*, written by the author, and professing that Pétrus Borel was dead, and that his real name had been Champavert. Some of the poems published two years before in the *Rapsodies* are quoted, and some biographical notes, not perhaps imaginary, are given. The rest of the book contains seven stories, named: *Monsieur de l'Argentière*, *l'Accusateur*, *Jaquez Banaon, le Charpentier* (La Havane), *Don Andrêa Vésalius, l'Anatomiste* (Madrid), *Three Fingered Jack, l'Obi* (La Jamaique), *Dina, la Belle Juive* (Lyon), *Passereau, l'Ecolier* (Paris), and *Champavert, le Lycanthrope* (Paris).

Each has a motto, or a series of mottoes, on the fly-leaf of its title, mostly from the Bible, and from contemporary poets, Gérard, Gautier, Musset. Each story is divided into a great number of divisions, and every division has its own title, more often in English, Spanish, Latin, or Provençal than in French. These seven stories, though not immoral, as they profess to be, in the defiant manner of the day, are as extraordinary as any production of the human brain. All are studies in horrors and iniquities; above all, in the shedding of blood. Written by anyone else they would be revolting, for they spare no detail of monstrous deeds; they would be pitiless but for their immense self-pity; cruel but for their irony, which is a bitter, personal, and at times magnificent arraignment of things. They are crude, extravagant, built up out of crumbling and far-sought materials; they are deliberately improbable, and the persons who sin and suffer in them are males all brain and females all idols and ideals. They are as far from reality as intention and style can make them; a world of vari-coloured puppets swinging on unregulated wires. And yet these violences and crudities and all this digging in graveyards and fumbling in the dead souls of the treacherous and the unforgiving, have something in them or under them, a sincerity, a real hatred of evil and unholy things, which keeps us from turning away, as our first impulse may well be, in mere disgust. A man, suffering from some deadly misery, leaps before us in ironical gymnastics, and comes down with his mortal laugh, a clown, in the arena. That is what makes the book tragic, a buffoon's criticism of life; there is philosophy in it, and an angry pathos.

Can the sense of horror become, to those accustoming themselves to it, a kind of luxury, like drunkenness? In another later book Borel tells us that it can: "Car il y a dans la douleur une volupté mystérieuse dont le malheureux est avide; car la souffrance est savoureuse comme le bonheur." Many great writers have had it, as a small part of their genius; Hugo had it, for instance, together with his passion for the tragically grotesque. But in this one writer horror seems to be almost the whole substance of his dreams. Whenever he seems about to open the door to beauty, horror shuts to the door. He does not suggest, he is minute, and will number every circumstance, which others would turn from. At times horror finds a voice in such a litany as Dina and the boatman chant on their dreadful voyage; or, with an appalling irony, in that scene where two negroes, fighting to death, stop suddenly at the sound of the convent bell striking eight, draw apart, kneel, repeat the "Angelus" each taking his turn, pray silently for one another's souls, and then rise and hack and tear each other to pieces. We shudder and wonder, and find the horror almost insupportable; but we do not, as in a story of Pierre Louÿs, sicken at the calm, deliberate cruelty of the writer. In Pétrus Borel horror is an obsession: its danger is at times to become an absurdity.

It is one of the defects of his hasty, defiant

art, that we are not always sure whether, when he is absurd, he is absurd intentionally. And it pleased him to write a style which was half splendour and half rage. Listen to this jewellery of the senses before Huysmans: "Depraved by grief, she sought ardently for all that irritated her nerves, all that excited and awakened her apathy; she covered herself with the most heavily scented flowers; she surrounded herself with vases full of syringa, jasmine, vervain, roses, lilies, tuberoses; she burned incense and benzoin; she shook around her amber, cinnamon, storax, musk." And he will tell you that a woman is "pyramidally virtuous"; and I hardly know how often things are *obombré*, which is the Biblical "overshadowed." English and Spanish rudely decorated his pages, generally more accurate than in the seekers after this form of local colour in his time. He has many varieties of dialogue from the pompous to the abject, but all are done with an uneven energy.

To be delivered from most of the beautiful as well as the discomforting things of the world, was the continual prayer of one who liked to be called "un lycanthrope." "La souffrance," he said, "a fait de moi un loup féroce," and the world to him was a thing "sur lequel je crache, que je méprise, que je répousse du pied." He realised that to think too closely about life was to be unhappy. And so that varying image of himself who goes through the best of his stories is the man who thinks and dies. What logic there is often in certain of the preposterous scenes, which reach their summit in the dialogue between the man who wants to be guillotined ("not publicly, but in your back garden") and M. Sanson, the state mechanician of the guillotine. The bourgeoisie itself is concentrated in one vast bewilderment in the professional gentleman who doubts, with strict politeness, the sanity of a strange visitor who addresses him after this manner: "Je jure par toutes vos oesophagotomies que j'ai mes saines et entières faculties; seulement, le service que je vous prie de me rendre n'est point dans les moeurs." But the one splendid, frantically original, sentence, which gives the whole accent to this strange story, is: "Peu de chose, je voudrais simplement que vous me guillotinassiez."

The whole story of *Passereau*, in which this

is the most significant of several audacious and unparalleled incidents, has a *macabre* humour which is terrible, if you will, but personal, and at that time new. It has been seen since, and we find Baudelaire, consciously or not, taking the exact details of his murderous drunkard's action, in *Le Vin de L'Assassin*, from the well in which Passereau drowns his mistress. The very words are almost the same. " Passereau alors," we read, "avec un grand effort, détache et fit tomber sur elle, une à une, les pierres brisées de la margelle," just as the drunkard in Baudelaire was to confess afterwards:

> Je l'ai jétée au fond d'un puits,
> Et j'ai même poussé sur elle
> Tous les pavés de la margelle.

Huysmans is anticipated, not only in such a passage as I have quoted, but in that sketch of an earlier des Esseintes: "Sometimes, the bad weather, having gone on without intermission, he remained cloistered for a whole month, surrounded perpetually by lamps, by torches, flooded by a splendid artificial daylight; reading, writing sometimes, but more often drunk or asleep. His door was closed against everyone but Albert, who came very readily, to shut himself up with him; not crazed by the same delirium, the same suffering, the same desolation, but for the oddity of the thing, for the chance of taking life in a wrong sense and of parodying this rectilineal bourgeoisie." Is it not almost to the very word characterising it, the plan of existence in *A Rebours?*

If a wild but living sketch may be compared, at whatever distance, with a flawless picture, it might be said that there is something in the power of creating a sense of suspense at the opening of a story, and in developing it to the explicit horror of the end, in which Pétrus Borel sometimes reminds us of Poe. Still more does he at times seem to anticipate Villiers de L'Isle-Adam. How like a first sketch of Villiers is the idea of suicide by guillotine, and the mock-pedantic form of the letter to the "Commission des Pétitions": "Dans un moment où la nation est dans la pénurie et le trésor phtisique au troisième degré, dans un moment où les délicieux contribuables ont vendu jusqu'à leurs bretelles pour solver les taxes, sur-taxes, contre-taxes, re-taxes, super-taxes, archi-taxes, impôts et contre-impôts, tailler et retailler, capitations, archi-capitations et avanies; dans un moment où votre monarchie obérée et votre souveraine piriforme branlent dans le manche, il est du devoir de tout bon citoyen," and so forth.

"To sing of love!" he says in the *Testaments*. It is a catalogue of his work; not Beddoes was more funereal. Is this obsession of blood, this continual consciousness of evil, this inability to see any but the dark contraries of things, a mere boastful affectation or the only possible way of expressing a personality so full of discontent, and bitter knowledge of reasoned complaint? All his stories have such a dissection, such a passing of all things through so bitter a crucible. "Pauvre Job au fumier," he calls himself in a poem, which seems to be sincere.

Pétrus Borel's next and last complete work, his "triste épopée," as he called it, was not published till six years after *Champavert*. The mood has again changed, or rather changes in the course of the interminable pages; the style is elaborated, and used with a singular, paradoxical effort. The name, *Madame Putiphar*, is of a nature to call up anticipations which are far from being gratified. Never was virtue so magnanimously or more preposterously presented, praised, and carried unshaken through unheard-of tribulations. Beings so transcendently moral and so consistently led by their merits and good deeds into pitfalls which the smallest worldly common-sense would have avoided, do not exist in fiction. A sentence in the book, not meant to refer to them, defines with perfect accuracy the manner of their treatment. "There are certain cases," we are told, "where really reason has so stupid an air, where logic has so absurd a figure, that one has to be extremely serious if one does not laugh in their faces." Is Deborah or Patrick MacWhyte the more saintly, the more heroic? It would be difficult to say, especially as, by a further freak of their chronicler, they are set for the most part to speak in a language so formal and artificial that the feeling it is meant to convey is only to be faintly seen through it. Here is Deborah speaking, at a moment of crisis, to her husband. "Veuillez croîre que je sais vous estimer," she says; "je ne suis point assez impertinente pour me supposer l'auteur de votre délicatesse et présumer que sans vos rapports avec moi vous eussiez été un malhonnête homme; mais, sans fatuité, il m'etoit bien permis de penser que, livré à vous-même, sans liens, sans serments, sans dilection emplissant votre coeur, placé dans la fatale alternative où vous vous êtes trouvé, vous auriez pu préférer manquer à l'exigence de vos vertueux principes," and much more: but no, the faultless man would have been quite capable of doing it all, on his own account. It is from the very explicit and perilous trial of his virtue by a Madame Putiphar who is meant to typify the worst side of the Pompadour that the book takes its name. Here, as elsewhere, the snares of evil are but vaunted to be trampled upon, and the pictures which are called up: "flowers, candles, perfumes, sofas, vases, ribbons, damask, a lovely voice, a mandoline, mirrors, jewels, diamonds, necklaces, rings, earrings, a lovely and gracious woman lying back languorously," are but the prologue to a condemnation.

The story itself begins with an arraignment of Providence, as if to justify the ways of man to God. "If there is a Providence, it often acts in strange ways! woe to him predestined to follow a strange way!" Such are these martyrs of their own virtue, and they are shown as, in a way, God's puppets. There is a sentence which might have been written by Thomas Hardy, so clearly does it state, in an image like one of his own, the very centre of his philosophy. "I have often heard that certain insects were made for the amusement of children; perhaps man also was created for the same pleasures of superior beings, who delight in torturing him, and disport themselves in his groans." There he states his own problem: the book is to be an illustration of it; hence the horrors and the angelic natures that endure them. But he has no explanation to give, and can but bow down, like a later mouthpiece of Villiers, "before the darkness."

It is from this gloomy and hopeless point of view that the whole horrors of the story are presented, up to page 250 of the second volume. Then, suddenly, comes a change of direction, and the last sixty out of the six hundred pages are written from this new point of view. "When I took up my pen to write this book my mind was full of doubts, of negations, of errors. But I know not by what mysterious means light has come to me on the way. I have constrained myself in the whole of this book to make vice flourish and dissoluteness overcome virtue; I have crowned roses with rottenness; I have perfumed iniquity with nard; I have poured overflowing happiness into the lap of infamy; I have brought the firmament down to the gutter; I have put dirt in the sky; not one of my brave heroes has not been a victim; everywhere I have shown evil as the oppressor and good as the oppressed." And now, he affirms, all these cruel accumulated destinies have turned upon him, after all his pains to interpret them, and have given him the lie.

"There is a Providence," he cries now, a God of Vengeance. The just man, if he suffers, suffers from some ancestral or attributed sin; and evil is destroyed by the action of God or some destroying power in man. "Croyez à un Dieu punisseur ici bas!"

he cries, or the world will be an enigma without a secret, an absurd, impossible charade. And he brings the great symbol of useful destruction, the French Revolution, to end his arraignment of the cruelty of things by a vengeance in which man takes back his rights, the sheep shearing the shearer, the people crushing its giants like a rag between its fists. And for him it is the approach of the hour when all those miseries that he has sung, and mountains more of them, shall weigh down the ultimate scale of the balances of the wrath of God.

In this sudden illumination, this prophetic outburst, which ends a book full of clouds, dissonances, errors, absurdities, but always sincere, noble or tending blindly towards nobility, we see certain brave and serious convictions underlying all that is contradictory and uncertain in a creature of passionate and eccentric imagination. When a people, he says, revolts against its deities, its first act is to break their images. That is what he does in these pages, where none of his deities are allowed to be logical.

A book so incoherent defies analysis, but it

is not difficult to see how closely the truth is followed in many of the details, the Defoe-like dungeon scenes, in particular, which are full of a painful reality, passing at least once, in the death-scene of Fitz-Harris, into notes as of an instrumental solo, as he cries in the last ecstasy of death in the pit's darkness, "All shines like a carbuncle; all is flaming, caressing, wavering, dusty."

For the actual part of these scenes Pétrus Borel has an invaluable model in the narrative of de Latude. No one, so far as I know, has identified the very striking resemblance between scenes in which, equally, we grope from horror to horror. My copy of *Le Depotism Dévoilé, ou mémoires de Henri Masers De Latude, détenu pendant trente-cinq ans dans divers prisons d'Etat*, is dated 1790, "imprimé aux frais de M. de Latude," and authenticated by his signature, in his own handwriting, at the foot of the preliminary *Avertissement*. All the names of the governors of the prison, and of fellow-prisoners are taken by Borel from de Latude, in one instance almost word for word: and the characterisation of Guyonnet, the first Governor of the Donjon of

Vincennes ("l'honnête M. de Guyonnet," as Borel calls him; "homme délicat et honnête," as he is called by de Latude), of Rougemont, his successor, who, in both narratives, is represented as the same odious tyrant, tampering with the prisoners' food, bricking up the little light left in their windows, suppressing their walks in the open air, "un sot, un fat, un puant, un pince-maille, un belître," as Borel calls him, is in both identical. The terrible lieutenant-general of police, defined by Borel as "un mauvais charlatan en manière de magistrate," is seen at much greater length in de Latude, who prints perhaps the most ghastly letter in the world. "Il feroit à-propos," he writes to the Minister, "de le transférer au Donjon de Vincennes, où il y a moins de prisonniers qu'à la Bastille, et de l'y oublier." In that phrase are exceeded all the horrors of *Madame Putiphar*.

Whatever was the good or evil reputation of the Pompadour who figures as Madame Putiphar in his pages, I find, in the evidently veracious and documented pages of de Latude, confirmation enough to justify that part of Borel's characterisation which is concerned

with her vindictive and destroying frivolity.
" What then has been my crime ? " de Latude
questions. " At the age of twenty-three years,
misled by an access of ambition which was
simply absurd, I displeased la Marquise de
Pompadour, I offended her, if you will, and
that is a good deal to admit. At forty years,
worn out by seventeen years of captivity and
of tears " :—but not yet nearly at the end of
either. And he affirms: " Also she has never
given liberty, as it is asserted, to any of those
whom she has hurled into chains; she shut
down for ever in the dungeon walls their sighs
and their anger." And he names (Borel names
them after him) a Baron de Venac, who was
imprisoned in the Donjon for nineteen years
for having given the Pompadour a piece of
good advice which "humbled her pride"; a
Baron de Vissec, seventeen years imprisoned
on the *suspicion* that he had spoken against
her; a Chevalier de Rochequerault, *suspected*
of being the writer of a pamphlet against her,
imprisoned for twenty-three years. Borel and
Latude's books, in scarcely less impressive
ways, represent the moment of her death, and
their natural hopes that a personal vengeance

would be set right at last by the law. "I
thought I saw the sky purple with shame,"
de Latude tells us. "Not even the idea came
to me that there could be any delay in breaking
my chains." For de Latude and for the
innocent prisoners of Borel no key unlocks
a door, and it is Borel who represents the
dying woman writing a great "no" in a last
refusal of mercy.

All this, then, and the episode of Malsherbes
visiting a prisoner in the pit of a dungeon,
drawing him up into the light, and then persuaded by false tidings to leave him to his
fate, is historical fact, and is used by Borel as
part of a story, which has so much of the
document where it seems most the invention
of a story-teller. Not less real, in its properly
artificial way, is the adventure of the Parc-
aux-Cerfs. Borel seeks too often such local
colour as "azederach," a Syrian tree, or the
plants "mahaleb" and "aligousier." Pedantry
comes in here as in other ways and places; as,
for instance, in the return to old spellings in
avoit, touts, abyme, gryllons. Pedantry passes
into ignorance in certain English words, which
we may set partly to the credit of those printers

NOTES ON PARIS AND
PAUL VERLAINE

THE ABSINTHE-DRINKER

Gently I wave the visible world away.
Far off, I hear a roar, afar yet near,
Far off and strange, a voice is in my ear,
And is the voice my own ? the words I say
Fall strangely, like a dream, across the day;
And the dim sunshine is a dream. How clear,
New as the world to lovers' eyes, appear
The men and women passing on their way!

The world is very fair. The hours are all
Linked in a dance of mere forgetfulness.
I am at peace with God and man. O glide,
Sands of the hour-glass that I count not, fall
Serenely: scarce I feel your soft caress,
Rocked on this dreamy and indifferent tide.

Boulevard Saint Germain.
 Aux Deux Magots.
  Paris, 1890.

PAUL VERLAINE

[To face p. 165.

I

AT THE CAFÉ FRANÇOIS PREMIER

LITERARY French Bohemia congregates in certain cafés of the Boulevard St. Michel—in the Café Vachette, the Soleil d'Or, the Café François Premier. When I was in Paris in 1890 it was at the François Premier that Verlaine had taken up his headquarters, possibly for no other reason than that it was near the hotel where he was then living. The café is situated high up the boulevard, at the less frequented end—just at the corner of the Rue Gay-Lussac. There I used to meet my friends the Décadents and the Symbolistes.

It is an evening in May: the clock points to half-past eleven. I am strolling along in front of the crowded cafés, watching all this delightful effervescence of life—the noisy, pleasant gaiety of the Boul' Mich' near midnight. Suddenly I hear a strident voice behind me: "Comment allez-vous, Monsieur Symons?" It is Jean Moréas. I turn, and he asks me to come with him to the café. Moréas is a Greek, and he has the dark features, blue-black hair, and half-savage, half-sullen black eyes which characterise the modern Athenian. An eternal monocle sticks jauntily in his eye. As we walk up the boulevard he begins to talk about his poems. At that time Moréas—who has since published a volume, *Le Pélérin Passionné*, which has given him a certain vogue—had published two volumes—*Les Syrtes* and *Les Cantilènes*. There is a slight but genuine inspiration in these fragmentary songs and ballads; one finds touches of naïve charm, a faintly fantastic grace, a quaint, archaic simplicity. I had just been reading the *Cantilènes*, and I told him how some of the pieces had charmed me. He began to recite, waving his arm and rolling out the consonants with all the emphasis of his iron voice. Moréas has two subjects of conversation, his own poems and *Hamlet*. He does not recite *Hamlet*, but the poems he recites at every opportunity, with a fine disregard of surroundings. I have heard him chanting them in a restaurant to the waitress, the charming Céline, surprised but impartial. In time we reach the Café François Premier, at the corner of the Rue Gay-Lussac. Voices hail us from a table to the right. There we find Charles Vignier, author of a book of verses called *Centon*, with his pale, elegant, perverse face, his blond plausiveness, always a veiled sneer about his lips. He is telling a dubious story, with a feigned air of remoteness, and the others are laughing. Opposite to him is Fernand Langlois, the young artist, whom I had met one memorable night at Verlaine's. He is incredibly tall and thin and youthful, with an air already of exhaustion, a tired grey look upon his features; he speaks in a soft, caressing, feminine voice, with the accents of a petted girl; he fixes large brown eyes upon you with a troubling intensity. Then there is a musician whose name I forget—it is not known to fame—a commonplace, bourgeois sort of person. And there are others, men who have printed and men who have only written verses. The conversation, out of compliment to me, turns upon English poetry. They are very anxious to know all I can tell them about Swinburne. Swinburne is well known by name in France, and since then an admirable prose translation of the *Poems and Ballads* has been made by Gabriel Mourey. They question me about Tennyson, about Browning, about Rossetti; they want to know who are the new poets, the new novelists; finally they insist on my repeating to them some English poetry, so that they may hear how it sounds—for none of them know English. Midnight has long past when the door is flung open, and Verlaine appears, followed by a noisy crowd of young men. Verlaine is leaning on his stick, his grey hat is pushed back, he gesticulates, explodes into conversation. When at last he can be prevailed upon to sit down, he too joins in the talk about things English. Verlaine at one time spent some years in England, and he is very proud of his knowledge of English. The conversation has become disjointed. Vignier, with his sceptical, ironical smile on his lips, is talking in a low voice to a man who sat down by his side; Moréas is thundering out some of his resonant verses, with that grand wave of the arm; more "bocks" are being ordered. And now all around there is a movement, a rattle of money, the sound of glasses being laid down, a hubbub of voices; men push past us on their way to the door, the women arrange their hats and nod farewells. It is closing time. "On ferme, Messieurs, on ferme!" shouts the *gérant*. Slowly, slowly, the unwelcome warning is obeyed. We are almost the last to go, and we file out, one by one, through the only door left open for our passage. In groups of two or three we stroll down the boulevard, refreshingly cool after the heated interior. I walk with Fernand Langlois, and we talk of art, of Gustave Moreau, of Puvis de Chavannes, of Burne-Jones, of Rossetti. One after another has dropped off, and when we come to the Rue Racine, I too say good-bye, and make my way homeward to my hotel under the shadow of the Odéon.

II
THE MAN

Not many years ago Paul Verlaine—whom serious critics are now beginning to speak of as the greatest living French poet—was almost unknown, even in France. An odd little circle of *Décadents* and *Symbolistes* had the wisdom to venerate him as a master, and the kindness to pay for his absinthe at the cafés. Certain writers, like Huysmans —independent of these narrow cliques—did something to widen a reputation which had so far been merely something vague, something rather scandalous. Then the Andrew Lang of Paris, Jules Lemaître, took up this more or less obscure writer and handsomely presented him to the boulevards. To-day they interview him in the *Figaro*, and the *Gaulois* tells you which hospital he is in at the moment.

The greatest living French poet I have called him, and I do not know whose claims can really be held to surpass the claims of the author of *Romances sans Paroles* and *Sagesse*. The former volume I remember seeing in Coppée's book-case, and I remember wondering whether Coppée had ever thought of Verlaine as a serious rival. Leconte de Lisle, Sully Prudhomme, Théodore de Banville—all admirable poets, each in his own very different way — all poets who have "succeeded," as it is called; but I for one would rather have written the little song of the wind—*Il pleure dans mon coeur*—than even *Un Acte de Charité*, than even *Le Vase Brisé*, than even the deftest of the *Odes Funambulesques*. The note of Verlaine's poetry is new in French verse; his form is new. For the first time the French language has become capable of all the delicate song-fulness of the English language; those stiff, impracticable lines which Victor Hugo bent, Verlaine has broken. His verse is as lyrical as Shelley's, as fluid, as magical—though the magic is a new one. It is a twilight art, full of reticence, of perfumed shadows, of hushed melodies. It suggests, it gives impressions, with a subtle avoidance of any too definite or precise effect of line or colour. The words are now *récherché*, now confidently commonplace—words of the boudoir, words of the street! The impressions are remote and fleeting as a melody evoked from the piano by a frail hand in the darkness of a scented room:

> Qu' est-ce que c'est que ce berceau soudain
> Qui lentement dorlote mon pauvre être?
> Que voudrais-tu de moi, doux chant badin?
> Qu' as-tu voulu, fin refrain incertain,
> Qui vas tantôt mourir vers la fenêtre
> Ouverte un peu sur le petit jardin?

Or, again, the impressions are as close and vivid as the circling flight of the wooden horses at the fair of St. Gilles, in Brussels:

> Tournez, tournez, bons chevaux de bois,
> Tournez cent tours, tournez mille tours;
> Tournez souvent et tournez toujours,
> Tournez, tournez au son des hautbois!

Or, again, they are as sharp, personal, and brutal as the song of prisoners turning "the mill of destiny":

> Allons, frères, bons vieux voleurs,
>   Doux vagabonds,
>   Filons en fleur,
>   Mes chers, mes bons ;
> Fumons philosophiquement,
>   Promenons-nous
>   Paisiblement;
>   Rien faire est doux.

The apparent contradiction between the exquisite and the brutal part of Verlaine's work—almost all of the work is exquisite—is simply the outcome of a temperament which has always been untamable, a career which has been impervious to every influence but the sudden, overwhelming influence of the moment—towards good, or towards evil. Paul Verlaine was born at Metz, March 30, 1844. His father, an officer, received his baptism of fire at Waterloo. Verlaine spent his childhood at Montpellier, was educated at Paris, and, at the age of twenty-three, brought out, under the wing of the *Parnasse Contemporain*, a volume of verse, *Poèmes Saturniens*. It was at the same time that Coppée published his first volume, equally unnoticed then, *Le Reliquaire*. Two years later Verlaine made a sort of literary success with the *Fêtes Galantes*. Next year, in 1870, occurred his unhappy marriage—a marriage at first all happiness—and it was in honour of his girl-wife that he published a tiny book of verse, *La Bonne Chanson*. When, four years later, the *Romances sans Paroles* appeared, Verlaine had already given way to every kind of self-indulgence, and with a sort of mad Bohemian gaiety was trailing a strange companion, the young poet, Arthur Rimbaud, over France, Brussels, Germany, and England. The pilgrimage was ended by a pistol-shot (I have heard Verlaine talk of it, very coolly) and for eighteen months Verlaine was in solitary confinement at Mons. He came out of prison a fervent Catholic, and after seven years' silence a volume of religious poems, *Sagesse* (1881)—one of the most sincere books ever written—was published obscurely at the office of a Catholic publisher named Victor Palmé. Verlaine's faith is unquestionably genuine, but it has never had a very appreciable influence upon his conduct. Always in misery, in penury, now lodging at the expense of his friends in some miserable *garni*, now, a little more comfortably and without expense, in hospital, he has published *Jadis et Naguère* (1884), a book of poems which represents every side of his work, *Amour* (1888), a pendant to *Sagesse*, and *Parallèlement* (1889), its antithesis. A volume of privately printed *Dédicaces* (sonnets to his friends) appeared in 1890, and he has written a book of criticism, *Les Poètes Maudits*, and one or two collections of tales in prose. A new volume of poems, *Bonheur*, long expected, appeared in 1891. *Bonheur*—Happiness—a strange title to be chosen by one who has apparently had so little of it, or who has grasped it with so feverish a haste as to crush it in the grasp. But Verlaine is perfectly aware of the many touches of irony which mark his strange career, and it was doubtless not without a consciousness of the full significance of the word that he named a volume of his poems *Sagesse*—Wisdom.

III
BONHEUR

SOME years ago, in a book rather of confession than of criticism, Paul Verlaine announced his intention (somewhat too formally, perhaps) of dividing his poetic work into two distinct sections, to be published in parallel series. *Sagesse*, *Amour*, *Bonheur*, were to "make for righteousness"; *Parallèlement* was to be frankly sensual; between them, he imagined, the whole man—that strange, composite, though not complex nature—would be fully and finally expressed. *Bonheur*, the third part, completing the trilogy, appeared in 1891.

Bonheur is written very much in the style of *Sagesse*, and a great part of it might be assigned, on internal evidence, to a period anterior to *Amour* and *Parallèlement*. It has none of the perversity, moral and artistic, of the latter book, despite a few experiments upon metre and rhyme. Nor is space devoted, as occasionally in *Amour*, to the mere courtesies of literary friendship. The verse has an exquisite simplicity, a limpid clearness, a strenuous rejection of every sort of artistic " dandyism "—the word is Verlaine's:

> et que cet arsénal,
> Chics fougueux et froids, mots secs, phrase redondante,
> Et cetera, se rende à l'émeute grondante
> Des sentiments enfin naturels et réels.

I take these lines from a poem which may be considered a new "Art Poétique." In that delicate and magical poem—itself the ideal of the art it sang—Verlaine said nothing about sincerity, except, inferentially, to the fleeting expression of something almost too vague for words. Music first of all and before all, and then, not colour, but the *nuance*, the last fine shade. Poetry is to be something intangible, a winged soul in flight "towards other skies and other loves." To express the inexpressible, he speaks of beautiful eyes behind a veil, of the full palpitating sunlight of noon, of the blue swarm of clear stars in a cool autumn sky; and the verse in which he makes his confession of faith has the exquisite troubled beauty—" sans rien en lui qui pèse ou qui pose "—which he commends as the essential poetry. Now, in this new poem of poetical counsel, he tells us that art should, first of all, be absolutely clear and sincere; it is the law of necessity, hard, no doubt, but the law:

> L'art, mes enfants, c'est d'être absolument soi-
> même.
> Foin! d'un art qui blasphème et fi! d'un art qui
> pose,
> Et vive un vers *bien* simple, autrement c'est la
> prose.

The verse in *Bonheur* is indeed "*bien* simple." There is a poem addressed to a friend—" Mon ami, ma plus belle amitié, ma meilleure "—which even Verlaine has hardly excelled in a kind of plaintive sincerity, full of the beauty of simple human feeling, seeking and finding the most direct expression:

> Aussi, précieux toi plus cher que tous les moi
> Que je fus et serai si doit durer ma vie,
> Soyons tout l'un pour l'autre en dépit de l'envie,
> Soyons tout l'un à l'autre en toute bonne foi.

NOTES ON PARIS AND PAUL VERLAINE 179

Verlaine speaks to his friend as if he would say more for friendship than has ever been said before. He would fain find words close and gracious enough to express all the intimacy and charm of their friendship:

> Elle verse à mes yeux, qui ne pleureront plus,
> Un paisible sommeil, dans la nuit transparente
> Que de rêves légers bénissent, troupe errante
> De souvenirs futurs et d'espoirs révolus.

"Remembrances to be, and hopes returned again"—how lovely a verse, French or English! And the emotion, temperate and restrained through most of the poem, rises at the end into exaltation:

> Afin qu'enfin ce Jésus-Christ qui nous créa
> Nous fasse grâce et fasse grâce au monde immonde
> D'autour de nous alors unis—paix sans séconde!—
> Définitivement, et dicte : Alleluia.

I quote this stanza not only because of its place in the poem—its expression of the culminating emotion—but because it is an excellent example of Verlaine's most characteristic technique. Note the rhyme at the beginning of the first line and at the end of the second, the alliteration, the curious effect produced by the repetition of "fasse grâce" (itself an assonance), the tormented rhythm throughout, the arbitrary and extraordinary position and transposition of accents. It cannot be said that all these experiences are always and equally successful; but it is useless to deny that Verlaine has widened the capacities of French verse. He has done what Goncourt has done in his prose: he has contributed to the destruction of a classical language, which, within its narrow limits, had its own perfection. But how great a gain there has been, along with this inevitable loss! In the hands of the noisy little school of *Décadents*, the brainsick little school of *Symbolistes*, both claiming Verlaine as a master, these innovations have of course been carried to the furthest limits of unconscious caricature. In Paris, a factitious clamour arose about a young Greek, Jean Moréas, a person who at one time had a very distinct talent for verse, which he wrote in regular metre, and without more of foreign idiom than his Athenian origin would lead one to expect. As one of his admirers calmly remarks, "il répudie toute règle préétablie pour la contexture de ses vers." From these extravagances Verlaine has always held aloof; and in an article published in 1890 he has given his opinion very frankly on those young *confrères* who reproach him, he tells us, " with having kept a metre, and in this metre some caesura, and rhymes at the end of the lines. *Mon Dieu!*" he adds, "I thought I had ' broken ' verse quite sufficiently." In *Bonheur*, for the first time in his work, there is one short poem—a concession to these young *confrères*—written in irregular unrhymed verse: verse, however, which is still verse, and not delirious prose. There are also two poems in assonant verse, one of them in lines of fourteen syllables, metrically quite regular. It is difficult to see any reason for the rejection of rhymes, but at all events they are rejected without disdain—frankly for a caprice.

Almost all the poems in *Bonheur* are closely personal—confessions of weakness, confessions of penitence, confessions of " l'ennui de vivre avec les gens et dans les choses," confessions of good attempts foiled, of unachieved resolutions. With a touch of characteristic self-criticism Verlaine says in one place:

> Mais, helas! je ratiocine
> Sur mes fautes et mes douleurs,
> Espèce de mauvais Racine
> Analysant jusqu'à mes pleurs.

And in its measure and degree this is true: there are times when confession becomes analysis, not to the advantage of the poetry. But, here as in *Sagesse*, the really distinguishing work is an outpouring of desires that speak the language of desire, of prayers that go up to God as prayers, not as literature; of confessions that have no reticences.

One of the finest pieces tells the story of that endeavour to rebuild the ruined house of life which Verlaine made at the time of his conversion, after those calm and salutary eighteen months of seclusion. This intensely personal poem, which is really a piece of the most exact autobiography, becomes a symbol of all lives that have fallen, that have struggled to rise, that have failed in the endeavour. Towards the end the emotion rises in a crescendo, half of despair, half of hope, as he cries out in the very fury of helplessness against the worst of foes—

> Vous toujours, vil cri de haro,
> Qui me proclame et me diffame,
> Gueuse inepte, lâche bourreau,
> Horrible, horrible, horrible femme!
>
> Vous, l'insultant mensonge noir,
> La haine longue, l'affront rance,
> Vous qui seriez le désespoir,
> Si la Foi n'était l'Espérance.
>
> Et l'Espérance le pardon,
> Et ce pardon une vengeance.
> Mais quel voluptueux pardon,
> Quelle savoureuse vengeance!

Elsewhere he writes of his life in hospital—"last home perhaps, and best, the hospital"; of his child-wife, for whose memory he has so strange a mixture of regretful complaint and unassuaged self-reproach; and always he returns to the burden of "Priez avec et pour le pauvre Lélian!"

IV

EPIGRAMMES

In this little book of *Epigrammes*, Verlaine tells us he has tried to do something of what Goethe did in the *Westoestlicher Divan*, but "en sourdine, à ma manière." And, indeed, there is a new note, as of a personality for once somewhat impersonal, concerned with general questions (always individually apprehended), with the interest of moral ideas, the charm of exterior things. The book was written in the calm retirement of that beautiful and fantastic hospital, Saint-Louis, which lies, like a little walled city of the middle ages, in the midst of the squalid and entertaining neighbourhood of the Canal Saint-Martin. It was written in a time of unusual quiet, written quietly, without excitement, and from memory, as one might say, a memory for once of the head, not of the heart or

NOTES ON PARIS AND PAUL VERLAINE 185

the senses. In the introductory verses we find already the real, evasive Verlaine, calming down, as he fancies or fears, to a certain indifference. "Les extrêmes opinions" of the past are to be more or less abandoned; as for the wiles of woman, "on finit par s'habituer"; the sharper clarion notes of the day — "le clairon fou de l'aurore" — fade into a dim fluting under the fading sunset; one is simply tired, and not too unwilling for sleep.

> Quand nous irons, si je dois encor la voir,
>   Dans l'obscurité du bois noir,
>
> Quand nous serons ivres d'air et de lumière
>   Au bord de la claire rivière,
>
> Quand nous serons d'un moment dépaysés
>   De ce Paris aux coeurs brisés,
>
> Et si la bonté lente de la nature
>   Nous berce d'un rêve qui dure,
>
> Alors, allons dormir du dernier sommeil!
>   Dieu se chargera du réveil.

This, then, is the note of the book; and in such a mood the memory of certain quaint or charming impressions comes up very happily. Japanese art, "lourd comme un crapaud, léger comme un oiseau": the *Ronde de Nuit*, seen at Amsterdam; Cazals' latest portrait of himself, the spectral back view which serves as frontispiece to the book; the haunting sound of a barrel-organ—

Bruit humain, fait de cris et de lentes souffrances
Dans le soleil couchant au loin d'un long chemin—

it is such sights and sounds as these that Verlaine evokes, in a series of delicately wrought little poems, more carefully written, for the most part, than much of his later verse. And there is one specially charming poem on the ballet:—

> Mon âge mûr qui ne grommelle
> En somme qu'encore très peu
> Aime le joli pêle-mêle
> D'un ballet turc ou camaïeu.

And the poem, if we mistake not, is a reminiscence of a certain memorable evening at the Alhambra, and it recalls quaintly, deliciously, a certain quaint and delicious paradox which summed up a personal and poetical view of life and art: "J'aime Shakspeare," said Verlaine, "mais j'aime mieux le ballet!"

V

CONFESSIONS

The *Confessions* of Verlaine — autobiographical notes from 1844, the year when he was born, to 1871, the year which proved the disastrous turning-point in his life — are quite unlike the confessions of anyone else, and have a charm of their own as individual as the charm of his verse. They tell, in a vague and yet precise way, in a manner of extreme simplicity which suggests even more than it says, and by means of a series of little facts, little impressions — "nuances presque infinitésimales qui ont, à mes yeux, leur importance très sérieuse" — the story of "une vie beaucoup en nuances." And they tell all this in an easy, casual manner (as it would seem), mainly by means of an extraordinary visual memory. "Les yeux surtout chez moi furent précoces: je fixais tout, rien ne m'échappait de formes, de couleurs, d'ombres. Le jour me fascinait et bien que j'étais poltron dans l'obscurité, la nuit m'attirait, une curiosité m'y poussait, j'y cherchais je ne sais quoi, du blanc, du gris, des nuances peut-être." The book, despite the deliberate evasiveness of its method: "n'importe, sans plus m'appesantir, tout simplement — en choisissant, élaguant, éludant? pas trop — m'y voici," is a subtle piece of psychology, the half-unconscious self-revelation of a man who has always been the creature of violent and uncertain instinct, who has never possessed himself, but who has always been curious as to his own qualities, not quite understanding them, and yet always so anxious to "confess." In this book, and not alone in the chapters relating to his childhood, he is always childlike in his frankness, his simplicity, and in the sincere, natural way in which he speaks of his follies and infirmities—"la manie, la fureur de boire," and the rest.

And in all the later part of the book, the story of his falling in love, his marriage, with but a hint of that "espèce d'enfer intermittent," which married life too soon became, there is an ingenuous directness which has again all the charm of a child's narrative of things. This love story (hinted at in *La Bonne Chanson*, which he tells us has always remained the dearest to him of his books) is one of the prettiest idylls of young love ever written. It is like nothing else in its intense humanity and its virginal delicacy. Of the more disorderly side of a life which was even then far from reticent, we hear but little: that little admirably precise, significant, and restrained. Nor does literature come very much into the scheme of these notes, though such indications as there are have a real biographical value, as, for instance, the story of how the literary instinct awoke, at the age of fourteen, with the surreptitious reading of Baudelaire's *Fleurs du Mal*, which the child was so far from understanding as to imagine even that the book "s'appelait tout bonnement: *Les fleurs de Mai*."

VI
DÉDICACES

VERLAINE's latest book of poems is truly described on the title-page as *nouvelle édition augmentée*. In its first, privately printed, edition, it was scarcely more than a pamphlet. In its final shape it is much the largest book that Verlaine has ever published. It is not one of the best, nor, indeed, could one expect it to be; for it is an informal bundle of friendly greetings, rather than a careful selection of verse, chosen for its own sake. In verse, much of which was written to order—at the order, that is, of a most friendly disposition—we are not likely to find the more poignant sentiment, or the more exquisite form, which we find in *Sagesse*, for instance, or in the *Fêtes Galantes*. On the contrary, it is only natural that one should come across many instances of that slovenliness of workmanship which mars so much of Verlaine's later work, in its exaggeration of certain curious virtues of style which he was one of the first to discover. For instance, there is the *enjambement*, or running of one line into another, to which Verlaine has been so singularly successful in giving just that air of choice simplicity which is one of the surprises of his manner of writing. Here, only too often, the lines run into one another merely because they happen to come in that way, with rhymes at the end of a certain counted number of syllables. Then the sonnets—the book is for the most part written in this form—are constructed after every shape, possible and impossible, in alternate short and long lines, in short lines with a long line at the end, in infinite malformations of rhyme-arrangement, and (I note with less regret) in that curious form, "la queue en l'air," which Huysmans compares to "certains poissons japonais en terre polychrome qui posent sur leur socle, les ouïes en bas." And, while few of the sonnets are without a touch of the familiar magic, there are not a few which have but one touch.

Yet, after all our reservations are made, the book contains a large amount of really excel-

lent work, and almost all of it is full of personal
interest, and, indeed, interest of various kinds.
What a medley of names I find here among
these *Dédicaces:* famous names, Coppée, Dierx,
Mallarmé, Huysmans, Léon Cladel, by the side
of anarchists after the order of Paterne Berri-
chon, eccentrics like Bibi-Purée, the fag and
butt of the Latin Quarter; then there is the
"cabaretier miraculeux" of the Chat-Noir,
Rodolphe Salis, and even the "Gérant du
Müller"; there are some doctors, a sculptor,
a musician, a painter; friends in London, with a
charming little miniature of Fountain Court:—

> La Cour de la fontaine est, dans le Temple,
> Un coin exquis de ce coin délicat.

And there are certain women, too, addressed
under discreet initials, now with little homely
details, as in the elegy on the death and funeral
of "E's" goldfinch—

> Tu repris, et cela me parut aussi beau:
> "Il aurait peut-être mieux fait sur mon chapeau!"—

or the even more charming poem on "Ph's"
little dog that died in babyhood, "Ses pattes
frêles en l'air, comme les oiseaux"; now more
intimately and more pathetically personal, as

> parceq'il faudrait une bienveillance
> à son propre égard, mais du
> fait que ce ne doit être d'abord
> qu'intime : un autre seul
> aura chargé de le définir et
> vous voulez bien être celui-là
> délicatement et magnifiquement.
> Rien, que j'aie voulu, sur
> quoi vous ne mettiez à coup
> sûr et comme une première fois
> le doigt.. Je presse la main
> entière. votre
>   Stéphane Mallarmé

FACSIMILE OF MS. BY STÉPHANE MALLARMÉ

[To face p. 192.

in the verses, "Encore pour G.," with their desolate ending:—

> Et je m'ennuie,—ainsi la pluie,
> Et je me pleure et je m'essuie
> Les yeux parce que je m'ennuie,
> Parce que je suis vieux et parce que je t'aime.

And, again, there are two splendid and resonant sonnets to Arthur Rimbaud, touched with that exaltation which informs everything that Verlaine writes of his dead friend; one of them, the first, being perhaps the finest poem in the book. In these sonnets the mainly familiar style is lifted, as it is also in the sonnet to Laurent Tailhade:—

> Le prêtre et sa chasuble énorme d'or jusques aux pieds—

where the words assume a sort of hieratic splendour, as of the very vestments they describe. Somewhat the same note reappears in the sonnet to Villiers de l'Isle Adam, and again in the early sonnet to Charles Morice—*Impérial, royal, sacerdotal*—which is reprinted, with five others, from *Amour*. This note, however, comparatively rare in Verlaine's work in general, is but seldom heard in these

Dédicaces. More really characteristic is the vaguely and singularly pathetic sonnet on Fernand Langlois:—

> Haut comme le soleil, pâle comme la lune,
> Comme dit vaguement le proverbe espagnol,
> Il a presque la voix tendre du rossignol,
> Tant son coeur fut clement à ma triste fortune.

And still more characteristic of the general tone of the volume is this brave, frank, open-air sonnet to Irénée Decroix:—

> Où sont les nuits de grands chemins aux chants bacchiques
> Dans les Nords noirs et dans les verts Pas-de-Calais,
> Et les canaux periculeux vers les Belgiques
> Où, gris, on chavirait en hurlant des couplets?
>
> Car on riait dans ces temps-là.—Tuiles et briques
> Poudroyaient par la plaine en hameaux assez laids;
> Les fourbouyères, leurs pipes et leurs bourriques
> Dévalaient sur Arras, la ville aux toits follets
>
> Poignardant, espagnols, ces ciels épais de Flandre;
> Douai brandissait de son côté, pour s'en défendre,
> Son lourd beffroi carré, si léger cependant;
>
> Lille et sa bière et ses moulins à vent sans nombre
> Bruissaient.—Oui, qui nous rendra, cher ami, l'ombre
> Des bonnes nuits, et les beaux jours au rire ardent?

It is this simpler, more easily good-humoured way of taking life, without asking too much or revolting too desperately, which is becoming Verlaine's final (dare one say final?) creed. Of a nature made up of so many irreconcilable elements, we get here mainly the less poignant side; not so much that

> Moi, l'ombre du marquis de Sade, et ce, parmi
> Parfois des airs naïfs et faux de bon apôtre,

but the facile, childlike part of that simplicity which can be so terribly and inconveniently in earnest. Here, then, for the present—for with Verlaine we can count only on the actual moment as it passes, not on any memory of the moment that has gone before, or any probability as to the moment that is to come after—here is the conclusion of the whole matter:—

> Bah! nous aurons eu notre plasir
> Qui n'est pas celui de tout le monde
> Et le loisir de notre désir.
>
> Aussi bénissons la paix profonde
> Qu'à défaut d'un tréssor moins subtil
> Nous donnerent ces ainsi soit-il.

VII

"INVECTIVES"

I NEVER read a book with more regret than this book of *Invectives*, which has appeared since the death of Verlaine. I do not see why it should not have been written, if the writing of a petulance helped to clear that petulance away. But what might have been a sort of sad or vexed amusement to Verlaine, in some sleepless hour in hospital, should never have been taken for more than what it was, and should never, certainly, have gone further than one of the best-locked cupboards in Vanier's publishing office. I should like to think that Verlaine never intended it to go further; and I am quite sure that, in the first instance, he never did intend it to go further. But I know Vanier, and I know that whatever Vanier got hold of he was not likely to lose Gradually the petulances would have heaped themselves one upon another, until they had come to about the size of a book. Then there would be the suggestion: why should we not make a book of them? Then jest would turn into earnest; Verlaine would be persuaded that he was a great satirist: it was so easy to persuade him of anything! And now here is the book.

Well, the book has some admirable things in it, and, as perhaps the most admirable, I will quote a piece called *Déception:*

> "Satan de sort, Diable d'argent!"
>   Parut le Diable
> Qui me dit: "L'homme intelligent
>   Et raisonnable,
>
> Que te voici, que me veux-tu?
>   Car tu m'évoques
> Et je crois, l'homme tout vertu,
>   Que tu m'invoques.
>
> Or je me mets, suis-je gentil?
>   A ton service:
> Dis ton voeu naïf ou subtil;
>   Bêtise ou vice?
>
> Que dois-je pour faire plaisir
>   A ta sagesse?
> L'impuissance ou bien le désir
>   Croissant sans cesse?

L'indifférence ou bien l'abus?
  Parle, que puis-je?"
Je répondis : "Tout vins sont bus,
  Plus de prestige,

La femme trompe et l'homme aussi,
  Je suis malade,
JE VEUX MOURIR." Le Diable: "Si
  C'est là l'aubade.

Qu tu m'offres, je rentre. En Bas.
  Tuer m'offusque.
Bon pour ton Dieu. Je ne suis pas
  A ce point brusque."

Diable d'argent et par la mort!
  Partit le Diable,
Me laissant en proie à ce sort
  Irrémediable.

In such a poem as this we have the Verlaine of the finer parts of *Parallèlement.* But what of the little jokes for and against M. Moréas, the pointless attack on Leconte de Lisle, the unworthy rage against M. Rod, the political squibs, the complaints against doctors and magistrates, the condescension to the manner of M. Raoul Ponchon? Here is neither a devouring rage, which must flame itself out, nor a fine malice, justifying its existence, as the serpent does by the beauty of its coils.

Verlaine's furies, which were frequent, were too brief, and too near the surface, to be of much use to him in the making of art. He was a big child, and his furies meant no more than the squalling and kicking of a baby. His nature was essentially good-humoured, finding pleasure on the smallest opportunity; often despondent, and for reasons enough, but for the most part, and in spite of everything —ill-health, poverty, interminable embarrassments—full of a brave gaiety. He often grumbled, even then, with a sort of cheerfulness; and when he grumbled he used very colloquial language, some of which you will not find in the dictionaries of classical French. These poems are his grumblings; only, unfortunately, they are written down, and we can read them in print, critically, instead of listening to them in sympathetic amusement. And what injustice they do him, alike as poet and man! How impossible it will be, now that this book has appeared, to convince anyone to whom Verlaine is but a name, that the writer of these *Invectives* was the most charming, the most lovable of men. The poet will recover from it, for, at all events, there are the *Fêtes Galantes*, the *Romances sans Paroles*, *Sagesse*, *Amour*, and the others, which one need but turn to, and which are there for all eyes. But the man!

Well, the man will soon become a legend, and this book will, no doubt, be one of the many contradictory chapters of the legend. In a few years' time Verlaine will have become as distant, as dubious, as distorted, as Gilles de Retz. He will once more re-enter that shadow of unknown horror from which he has but latterly emerged. People will refuse to believe that he was not always drunk, or singing *Chansons pour elle*. They will see in his sincere Catholicism only what des Esseintes, in the book of Huysmans, saw in it: "Des rêveries clandestines, des fictions d'un amour occulte pour une Madone byzantine qui se muait, à un certain moment, en une Cydalise égarée dans notre siècle." And they will see, perhaps, only a poetical licence in such lines as these, in which, years ago, Verlaine said all that need ever be said in excuse, or in explanation of the problem of himself:

Fountain Court.

à Arthur Symons.

La "Cour de la fontaine" est, dans le Temple,
Un coin exquis de ce point délicat
Du Londres vieux où le jeune avocat
Apprend l'étroite Loi, puis le Droit ample ;

Des arbres moins anciens (mais vieux, sans faute)
Que les maisons d'aspect ancien si bien
Et la noire chapelle au plus ancien
Encore galbe, — aujourd'hui .. table d'hôte !

Des moineaux francs picorent joliment
— Car c'est l'hiver — la baie un peu moisie
Sur la branche précaire, et — poésie !
La jeune Anglaise à l'Anglais agréément.

Qu'importe ! Ils ont raison, et nous aussi,
Symons, d'aimer les vers et la musique
Et tout l'art, et l'argent mélancolique
D'être si vite envolé, vil souci !

" Et

FACSIMILE OF MS. BY PAUL VERLAINE

[*To face p.* 200.

« Et le jet d'eau ride l'humble bassin »
Comme chantait, quand il avait votre âge,
L'auteur de ces vers-ci, débris d'orage,
Ruine, épave, au vague et lent dessin.

Le 7 février 1894

P. Verlaine

Un mot encore, car je vous dois
Quelque lueur en définitive
Concernant la chose qui m'arrive :
Je compte parmi les maladroits.

J'ai perdu ma vie et je sais bien
Que tout blâme sur moi s'en va fondre :
A cela je ne puis que répondre
Que je suis vraiment né Saturnien.

A PRINCE OF COURT PAINTERS

A PRINCE OF COURT PAINTERS

ALL Watteau is in that *Imaginary Portrait* which Walter Pater wrote in the form of extracts from the diary of Watteau's neighbour and friend at Valenciennes, the daughter of Antoine Pater, "maître sculpteur," and the sister of Jean Baptiste Pater, Watteau's only pupil. The family of Walter Pater came from that part of Flanders, and was, indeed, closely connected with the family of the painter, and in writing these extracts from the diary it amused him to reconstruct what might well have been some of his family papers. For the facts of Watteau's life he went to the carefully documented essay of the Goncourts, and especially to the contemporary narrative which they printed from a MS. In the new life of Watteau, by M. Virgile Josz, we have for the first time a quite trustworthy biography, in which some new facts are established and some slight but important corrections made. How well M. Josz knows the life and art of the 18th century his previous study of Fragonard has already shown. His new book has the charm of a brilliant historical novel, and it is everywhere founded upon precise documents. He has the art of weaving a narrative full of colour, full of picturesque detail, in which careful research and subtle criticism become part of an unfatiguing entertainment. No really serious critic and historian of art at the present day has so light a touch, so easy a mastery over his material. And, after reading this minute, learned, and sympathetic study of *le plus grand, le plus mystérieux, le plus troublant génie du xviiie siècle*, one still finds, on turning to Pater's *Prince of Court Painters*, that all Watteau is there, divined, analysed, praised faultlessly, in that hardly imaginary portrait.

Watteau went through life like one always in hiding, sick, restless, distrustful; unsatisfied with himself and his work; never really at home in the world. His malady drove him from place to place, in an unsuccessful search after tranquil obscurity, in the incessantly renewed hope of some new place in which he could be perfectly well, not distracted by friends or by cares, alone with his work. From his youth he was weary of most pleasures, most desires; always a critic, and most of that which he cared most to render. It was his delight and his labour to look on at a life which was not his, and in which he did not desire to mingle. He is himself that melancholy spectator of pleasures in which he does not share, whom he has placed in the corner of so many of his pictures; or *l'Indifferent*, poised for the dance to which he brings an aged smile and a joyless knowledge of the steps of the measure. He creates the most exquisite woman in modern painting, and goes through life with a careful withdrawal from too close a contact with women. The painter of *fêtes galantes*, he is never the dupe of those sentimental reveries in which there is no frank abandonment of the flesh or spirit. His brush has both coquetry and raillery, and no wit in paint was ever so discreet in its comments on life,

Watteau is the only painter of *la galanterie*

who has given seriousness to the elegance of that passing moment, who has fixed that moment in an attitude which becomes eternal. And he has done so alike by his intellectual conception of life, of the human comedy, and by the distinction, the distinguished skill of his technique. For a similar gravity in the treatment of "light" subjects, and for a similar skill in giving them beauty and distinction, we must come down to Degas. For Degas the ballet and the café replace the Italian comedy of masks and the afternoon conversation in a park. But in Degas there is the same instantaneous notation of movement and the same choice and strange richness of colour; with a quite comparable fondness for seizing what is true in artificial life, and what is sad and serious in humanity at play. But Watteau, unlike Degas, is never cruel. He has almost an envy of these elegant creatures, and of their capacity for taking no thought for the morrow; he, as he gives them immortality, thinks sadly of the temporary joys. He listens to the same music, sees their hands and lips join, and is himself never ready for that *Embarquement pour Cythère* towards which he sees them moving. It is with disillusioned, not with mocking, eyes that he looks upon those to whom the world is still unspoilt. Happy are those, he seems to say, who can be happy.

Watteau was a great lover of music, and he has placed instruments of music even in hands that do not know how to hold bow and handle. Like music, his painting is a sad gaiety, and I rarely look at his pictures without receiving almost a musical sensation. It is a music of lute and clavichord, in which the strings sob and the quills rustle, and sometimes one may say, as Browning says of Galuppi: "In you come with your cold music till I creep through every nerve."

There is a certain chill in this music of the pictures which could never, unlike the music itself, have sounded merry when Gilles and Finette were alive. The colour of Watteau is always the colour of bright things faded, of rose-petals in the old age of roses. There is melancholy in the subdued grace of his lines, full of active languor. And in his women, themselves like a delicate music, there is something almost disquieting, some of the mystery of music.

For Watteau a woman is the most beautiful thing in the world; something of a toy, perhaps, or an ornament, flowers or jewels; and her clothes must be as beautiful as herself. He paints what no one else has painted: a *frisson* made woman. But he paints without desire, with a kind of tender, melancholy respect for the soul of the flesh, embodied in fine silks, fragile, loving to be loved. For him she is a bibelot, not a mistress, and he has made her after his own heart. He paints her cheek and her face with the same tenderness, the same passionate ecstasy. And he has put into her eyes not only that dainty malice with which she fights and conquers, but also that dainty mystery with which she attracts and retains.

The woman of Watteau is woman clothed and civilised, and in the best society. Born a mason's son, he had, all his life, an instinctive aversion for *la bas peuple;* the people through whom one must elbow one's way. And his women, if they are not in fancy dress, and playing romantic parts, are always women who have the leisure to be beautiful, to play at life. The Frenchwoman begins to exist in his pictures, and he has fixed a type, which remains what most Frenchwomen would wish to be. These piquant, enigmatical creatures have supreme worldly elegance. The suspicion of thought which he has hinted at in their swift eyes is a reticence which would promise and remain free. They have the mystery which a woman has for a man, because he is a man and she a woman.

With Watteau Flemish painting ends and French painting begins. He was a devout student of Rubens, and learnt from him various secrets, a different but not lesser life of the flesh, a more tempered but not less splendid life of the clothes. He adds as much in elegance as he omits in amplitude; he creates a new thing, which is French. And may it not be said, with M. Josz, that he does more than anyone has yet done towards the creation of English painting? In that year which he spent in London, just before his death, his work had an immediate and an immense success. When Frederick the Great, twenty years after his death, wanted to buy some of his pictures, his intendant answered: "Tous les ouvrages que Watteau à fait sont presque tous en Angleterre, où on en fait un cas infini." Holbein, Rubens, Vandyke, had been in England, had painted there, been admired; but it is only after the visit of Watteau and the sight of this delicacy, finesse, this clear and vaporous colour, this arresting of fine shades, this evocation of a new, sensitive, modern beauty, that the English begin to paint; and are there not in the work of Watteau qualities which anticipate Reynolds and Gainsborough, as there are qualities which anticipate both Constable and Turner?

1903.

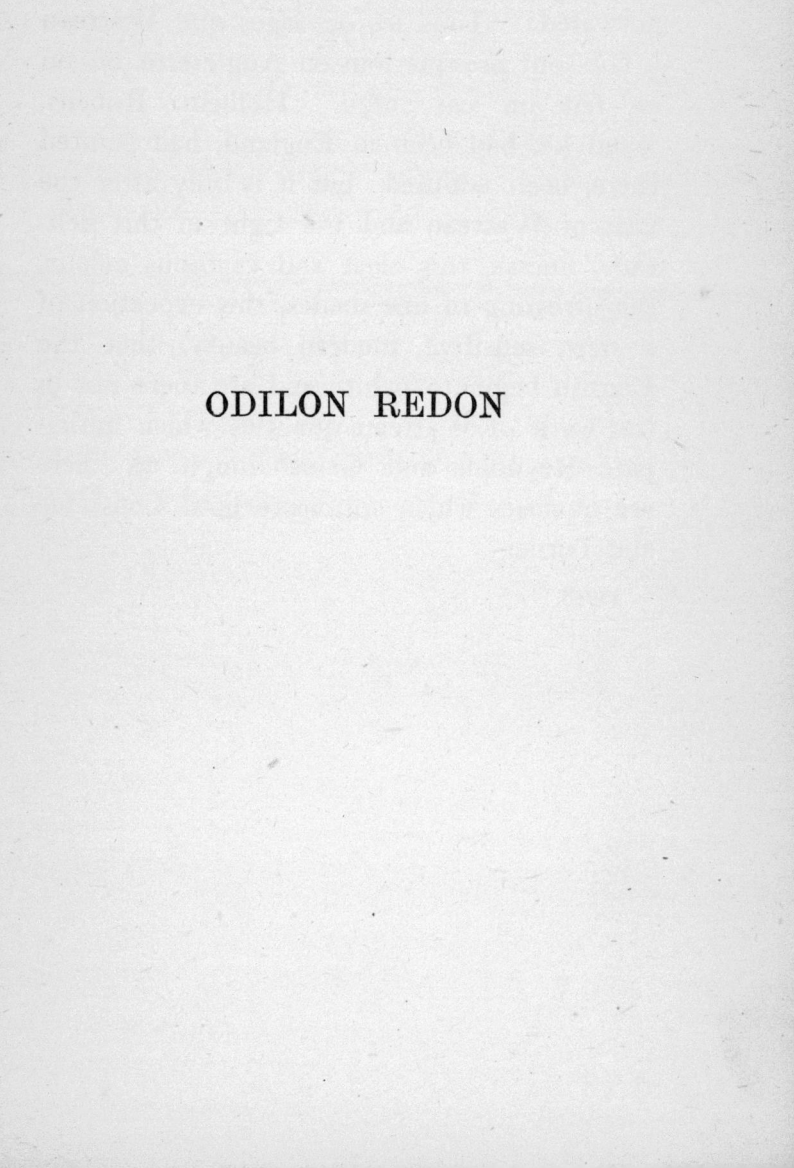

ODILON REDON

ODILON REDON

THE name of Odilon Redon is known to but few people in France, and to still fewer people in England. Artistic Paris has never had time to think of the artist who lives so quietly in her midst, working patiently at the record of his visions, by no means discouraged by lack of appreciation, but probably tired of expecting it. Here and there the finer and more alert instinct of some man who has himself brought new gifts to his art—Huysmans, Mallarmé, Charles Morice, Emile Hennequin—has divined what there is of vision and creation in this strange, grotesque world which surges only half out of chaos—the world of an artist who has seen day and night.

The work of Odilon Redon—his later work, that which is most characteristic of him—

consists of a series of lithographic albums, all published since 1880: *Dans le Rêve, À Edgar Poe, Les Origines, Hommage à Goya, La Tentation de Saint Antoine, À Gustave Flaubert, Piéces Modernes*, and *Les Fleurs de Mal*. Each album contains from six to ten plates in large folio, printed on *beau papier de Chine*, without text, often without title, or with a vague and tantalising legend, such as *Au réveil, j'aperçus la Déesse de l'Intelligible, au profil sévère et dur*. So, without an attempt to conciliate the average intelligence, without a word of explanation, without a sign of apology for troubling the brains of his countrymen, Odilon Redon has sent out album after album. So little effect have they produced that it has taken ten years to sell twenty-four out of the twenty-five copies of *Dans le Rêve*. "Reste l'exemplaire."

Odilon Redon is a creator of nightmares. His sense for pure beauty is but slight, or rather for normal beauty; for he begets upon horror and mystery a new and strange kind of beauty, which astonishes, which terrifies, but which is yet, in his finest work, beauty all the same. Often the work is not beautiful at all: it can be hideous, never ineffective. He is a genuine visionary: he paints what he sees, and he sees through a window which looks out upon a night without stars. His imagination voyages in worlds not realised, voyages scarcely conscious of its direction. He sees chaos, which peoples its gulfs before him. The abyss swarms—*toutes sortes d'effroyable bêtes surgissent*—animal and vegetable life, the germs of things, a creation of the uncreated. The world and men become spectral under his gaze, become transformed into symbols, into apparitions, for which he can give no account often enough. *C'est une apparition—voilà tout!* He paints the soul and its dreams, especially its bad dreams. He has dedicated some of his albums to Flaubert, to Poe, to Baudelaire; but their work is to him scarcely so much as a starting-point. His imagination seizes on a word, a chance phrase, and transforms it into a picture which goes far beyond and away from the author's intention—as in the design which has for legend the casual words of Poe: " L'œil, comme un ballon bizarre, se dirige vers l'infini." We see an actual eye and an actual balloon : the thing is grotesque.

The sensation produced by the work of Odilon Redon is, above all, a sensation of infinitude, of a world beyond the visible. Every picture is a little corner of space, where no eye has ever pierced. Vision succeeds vision, dizzily. A cunning arrangement of lines gives one the sense of something without beginning or end: spiral coils, or floating tresses, which seem to reach out, winding or unwinding for ever. And as all this has to be done by black and white, Redon has come to express more by mere shadow than one could have conceived possible. One gazes into a mass of blackness, out of which something gradually disengages itself, with the slowness of a nightmare pressing closer and closer. And, with all that, a charm, a sentiment of grace, which twines roses in the hair of the vision of Death. The design, *La Mort*, is certainly his masterpiece. The background is dark; the huge coils which terminate the body are darker than the background, and plunge heavily into space, doubling hugely upon themselves, coils of living smoke: yet the effect of the picture is one of light—a terror which becomes beautiful as it passes into irony. The death's head, the little vague poverty-stricken face, is white, faint, glimmering under the tendrils of hair and roses: tresses of windy roses which stream along and away with an effect of surprising charm, the lines running out in delicate curves, to be lost in the night. And below, separated from the head by a blotch of sheer blackness, one sees a body, a beautiful, slender supple body, glittering with a strange acute whiteness, with a delicate arm raised to the empty temples of the skull. Below, in its frightful continuation of the fine morbid flesh of the body, the black column, the huge and heavy coils, which seem endless. The legend is from Flaubert. Death speaks, saying: *Mon ironie dépasse toutes les autres.*

Ammonaria and *Le Sphinx et la Chimère* are from the same album, which illustrates *Le Tentation de Saint Antoine*, and are characteristic, though not the finest, examples of Redon's work. The scene of

Ammonaria is before the temple of Serapis, at Alexandria. It is a Christian martyr whom they are scourging: she writhes under the blows, in the cruel sunlight: one feels the anguish of the bent and tortured figure, suffering visibly. The other design renders that marvellous dialogue between the Sphinx and the Chimera. "C'est que je garde mon secret!" says the Sphinx. "Je songe et je calcule. . . . Et mon regarde que rien ne peut dévier, demeure tendu à travers les choses sur un horizon inaccessible. Moi," replies the Chimera, "je suis légère et joyeuse!" and it is a veritable hilarity that one discovers, looking at it rightly, in the regard of the strange creature: a spasm of ironic laughter in the blots of blackness which are its eyes, in the mouth that one divines, in the curl and coil of the whole figure. In the calm gaze and heavy placid pose of the Sphinx, lines of immeasurable age above its eyes, there is a crushing force which weighs on one like a great weight, something external. The power of the Chimera is of the mind and over souls. Vague, terrible, a mockery, a menace, it has the vertigo of the gulf in its eyes, and it draws men toward those "new perfumes, those larger flowers, those unfelt pleasures," which are not to be found in the world. In another design the Chimera, spitting fire from its nostrils, light glittering and leaping on wings and tail, turns on itself, distending its jaws in a vast ironic bark: *la chimère aux yeux verts, tournoie, aboie*. More terrible, more wonderful, more disquieting is *Le Diable avec les sept Péchés cardinaux sous ses Ailes*. The design is black upon black, and it is only slowly that a huge and solemn, almost a maternal face, looms out upon one: Satan, placid, monstrous, and winged, who cradles softly the little vague huddled figures of the seven deadly sins, holding them in his large hands, under the shadow of his wings. And there is another Satan, valiantly insurgent against the light that strikes him, a figure of superb power in revolt. Yet another design shows us Pegasus, his beautiful wing broken, a wing that had felt the high skies, falling horribly upon the rocks: all the agony and resistance of the splendid creature seen in the trampling hoofs and heaving sides, and the head caught back by the fall. Again one sees a delicate twilight landscape of trees and birds, a bit of lovely nature, and in it, with the trouble of a vague nightmare, coming there inexplicably, *Le Joueur*, a man who holds on his shoulders an immense cube painfully: the man and the trees seem surprised to see each other. There is another landscape, a primeval forest, vague and disquieting, and a solitary figure, the figure of a man who is half a tree, like some forgotten deity of a lost race: the forest and the man are at one, and hold converse. And there are heads, heads floating in space, growing on stalks, couched on pedestals; eyeballs, which voyage phantasmally across the night, which emerge out of nests of fungus, which appear, haloed in light, in the space of sky between huge pillars; there are spectral negroes, there are centaurs, there are gnomes, a Cyclops (with the right accent of terrifying and yet comic reality), embryonic formless little shapes, and, persuasively, the Sciapodes of Flaubert: "La tête le plus bas possible, c'est le secret du bonheur! Il y doit avoir quelque part," says Flaubert, "des figures primordiales, dont les corps ne sont que les images," and Redon has drawn them, done the impossible. . The Chimera glides mystically through the whole series. Death, the irony; Life, the dream; Satan, the visible prince of darkness, pass and repass in the eternal dance of apparitions.

1903.

Printed in Great Britain by
Richard Clay & Sons, Limited,
Brunswick St., Stamford St., S.E. 1,
and Bungay, Suffolk.